Jessie Benton

FRÉMONT

ISBN 978-1-893103-33-7
Library of Congress Control Number: 2008941519

Published in the United States of America by:
Beautiful Feet Books
1306 Mill Street
San Luis Obispo, CA 93401
www.bfbooks.com
1.800.889.1978

ABOUT THE AUTHOR
MARGUERITE HIGGINS
1920-1966

MARGUERITE HIGGINS CAME TO HER SUBJECT OF THE
life of Jessie Benton Fremont quite naturally as the two
women, though separated by a century, shared much in
common. Both were gifted writers with a keen intelligence and a love of adventure. Neither feared challenging the proscribed roles of women in their day and their
mutual intrepidness resulted in significant contributions
to history as it unfolded in both the nineteenth and
twentieth centuries.

Marguerite was born on September 3, 1920, in
Hong Kong where her father was working in the ship-
ping industry. Her American father served as a pilot in
France during World War I where he met and married a
French woman, Marguerite Goddard. The family returned to California where Marguerite eventually won a
scholarship to the Anna Head School in Berkeley. She
later attended the University of California at Berkeley
where she graduated with honors in journalism in 1941.
She then completed a master's program in journalistic
studies at Columbia University while working as a col-
lege correspondent for the New York Tribune.

America's involvement in World War II meant
that many men left jobs to join the armed forces, provid-
ing Higgins with an opportunity to fulfill her dream of
war correspondent. She was finally assigned to London
in 1944, but still longed for front line action and after
much persistence was allowed to go to Paris on assignment. Higgins was there for the fall of Munich and was

one of a group of reporters that toured war ravaged Germany and witnessed the liberation by Allied troops of both Dachau and Buchenwald Nazi concentration camps. Indeed, she and her colleague actually arrived at Dachau ahead of Allied troops and took surrender of that camp from SS agents. Her firsthand accounts of these events were front-page articles in the New York Herald Tribune.

After the war Higgins became bureau chief in Berlin and covered the Nuremberg War Trials and witnessed the growing tensions between east and west. Her time there strengthened her growing anti-Communist sentiment, as she ultimately became convinced that America needed to fight the spread of communism worldwide.

In 1950 Higgins was transferred to the Tokyo office and quite propitiously, was there when North Korea invaded South Korea. Shortly after war broke out, General Walton W. Walker expelled all female journalists from the country. But Higgins, never one to walk away from a good story, or a good fight, somehow convinced General Douglas MacArthur to rescind this ruling; the Herald received his wire stating, "Ban on women in Korea lifted. Marguerite Higgins held in highest esteem by everyone." These events became material for her highly acclaimed book *War in Korea*. For her war correspondence from Korea, Higgins became the first woman to receive the Pulitzer Prize in international reporting.

In 1953 Higgins was sent to Vietnam where she covered the fall of the French Army at Dien Bein Phu. Her articles expressed her strongly anti-Communist sentiments earning her the scorn of younger liberal journalists. While reporting from the front lines, Higgins narrowly escaped death when the photographer Robert Capra, whom she was walking beside, was killed by a land mine. Her concern about military involvement in Vietnam prompted her book, *Our Vietnam Nightmare* (1965). On one of her last trips there, she contracted the tropical fever leishmaniasis, returned to the United States to recover, but died on January 3, 1966 at the age of 45. For her service to her country as a journalist and war correspondent, she was buried at Arlington National Cemetery.

Marguerite Higgins elevated the world of women's journalism by her spunk, tenacity, and devotion to excellence in international reporting. As the first woman to receive the Pulitzer Prize in this field, she inspired women around the world. Her eyewitness accounts of some of the century's most seminal events continue to provide an important window into the geopolitical history of a turbulent era.

--Rea Berg, 2008

Other works by Marguerite Higgins:

Red Plush and Black Bread (1955)
News is a Singular Thing (1955)
War in Korea—Report of a Woman Combat
Correspondent (1951)
Our Vietnam Nightmare (1965)

CONTENTS

It requires two types of talent to make any adventure memorable: the bravery to live it, and the literary skill to report it. It took Agamemnon, Achilles, and their fellow heroes to win the Trojan War. But without the poet Homer, their deeds might have been forgotten.

By happy coincidence, both types of talent were present in the union of John Charles Frémont and his wife Jessie. He was the pathfinder across our pathless western wilderness. She was the talented writer who polished into prose the rough notes and scientific data he brought back from each of his expeditions. The great success of their books came from their harmonious partnership: his courage and her writing talent.

Marguerite Higgins, whose own deft pen aided our armed might in Korea, instinctively understands the role of Jessie Frémont, who inspired her husband, defended him against his enemies, and transformed his adventures into literature.

Let us offer a tribute to all who defend our country with sword or pen. May our powder stay dry and our typewriters well oiled in the challenging years that lie ahead!

STERLING NORTH
General Editor

Jessie Benton

FRÉMONT

1

"Hurrah for Jackson"

"WHO led in this thing?"

Tom Benton's voice was stern as he looked at the papers on his desk. A few moments before, when he left the library on a brief errand, the papers were stacked in a neat pile, the finished manuscript of a speech he would deliver in the United States Senate. Now they were in disarray and smeared with colored chalk.

Behind the desk sat Jessie Anne Benton, a girl of six, and standing at her side was her sister Eliza, eight. The corners of their mouths were discolored from licking the crayons before making their childish scrawls. They were dressed in bright new coats and bonnets for an afternoon walk around Lafayette

Square with their father, and their coats bore marks
of chalk dust.

Jessie and Eliza were startled by the seldom-
heard anger in their father's voice. Thomas Hart
Benton could shake the rafters of the Senate cham-
ber with his oratory, but at home he spoke in the
mildest tone, except on rare occasions. This was one
of them, and Eliza, in shame and fright, began to
weep. Jessie's resourceful mind was too busy for
tears.

For months she had been fascinated by the
street crowds of Washington shouting "Hurrah for
Jackson." She remembered the pleasure her father
had shown when Andrew Jackson was sworn in as
President of the United States a few months earlier.

"Who led in this thing?"

Jessie lifted her brown eyes to the stern gaze of
her father, still waiting for an answer, and solemnly
replied: "A little girl that says 'Hurrah for Jackson.' "

Tom Benton fought back a smile. If he had in
mind punishing the girls, Jessie's clever confession
stopped him. All he could do was to correct her
grammar and gently send the sisters out to wash
their faces for the stroll in the park.

Benton was to remember fondly one paragraph
that Jessie had smudged with her blue crayon be-

cause it foretold the struggle for the West that would be an important part of his daughter's adult life. As a Senator from Missouri, Benton had prepared the speech in answer to another senator's bill that would deny public lands to future settlers. The paragraph read:

> The West is my country, not his. I know it; he does not. It is an injury to the human race to undertake to preserve the magnificent valley of the Mississippi for the haunts of wild beasts instead of making it the abode of liberty and civilization, an asylum for the oppressed of all nations.

If her father seemed indulgent toward Jessie, it was because he saw in her qualities of his own. She was curious about the whole world, frank and fearless beyond her years. While her mother fretted over the frail Eliza and took care of her infant son Randolph, Jessie became the special charge of her father. She preferred his company, and he in turn realized that a child so independent-minded and strong-willed needed a firm guiding hand. He spent many hours as her teacher.

Visitors to the Benton library often found little Jessie sprawled on the red carpet near the fireplace,

illustrated volumes of history and travel open before her. While she waited for her father to resume her instruction, she would spell out words aloud with an astonishing self-reliance for a girl of six.

Even when the Benton family required the Senator to employ a private tutor, Jessie invented excuses to carry her exercise books into the library, where her patient father had installed a chair near his own so that they could study and talk about the child's endless interests.

The tutor, a Polish gentleman named John Sobieski who lived in the big house, taught music, history and French. He was constantly amazed by Jessie's fund of knowledge, picked up in her daily walks and talks with her father.

Once when the children were going through their history lesson, Jessie interrupted the tutor and began to talk about truffles, which are a kind of mushroom. The Greeks, she said, thought truffles were created by thunder because they were black. But they really grew like small potatoes at the roots of hazel trees in France and were dug up by trained "truffle dogs," she explained.

"What has this to do with history, Miss Jessie?" the exasperated tutor asked.

Surprised by his tone, Jessie replied firmly, "I was telling you the history of truffles."

Sobieski on another occasion took Jessie and sisters (now including Sarah and Susan as well as Eliza) to a benefit concert at an orphanage in Georgetown. As the orphans entered singing a hymn, Jessie tugged at the tutor's sleeve and whispered, "Do they have to praise God for making them orphans?"

That evening, after dinner, Jessie was silent while her sisters talked about the refreshments served at the orphanage. Finally she blurted out, "Oh, Father, I didn't know there were that many orphans in the whole world! Surely there can't be love enough to go round in such a place."

As Mrs. Benton spoke of the kindness of the nuns who ran the orphanage, Tom Benton could only look in wonder at his compassionate daughter, silently contemplating her solemn brown eyes and the red-brown curls and the delicately molded face that seemed at once so innocent and wise.

On many days, Jessie went with her father to the Capitol and while he attended to his official duties, was left in the Congressional Library under the kindly care of a Mr. Meehan, the librarian. She sat before the low bookstands and leafed through volumes of Audubon's *Birds* and illustrated travels. At noon, a servant would come for her. And during her afternoon walks with her father, she was encouraged to tell him what she had learned.

She mixed her tales with childish fact and fancy, describing Audubon's works as a pair of love birds swaying on a birch twig or a hummingbird on a blade of grass, telling about a camel train moving out into the desert.

One day she persuaded her father to make an eerie promise. Walking along the Potomac River, she came upon the skeleton of a small bird lying in the grass. She picked it up and studied it thoughtfully, then laid it down again and turning to her father, said:

"When I die, don't bury me in a box. Lay me in a bed of violets, for I want the flowers to grow up through my bones."

Tom Benton solemnly agreed to the request of his strange, enchanting daughter, too wise a parent to spoil her wondrous love for nature with even a smile.

To others, President Jackson was a rough-hewn man, hard in the ways of frontier politics and not much impressed by the fancy social life of Washington's salons. He had many enemies and was pictured without sentiment. But Jessie Anne Benton knew better.

Her father frequently took her along to the White House for visits with the President, who had helped Benton establish himself as a lawyer in the territory of Missouri in 1815. Before that, Benton had spent much time at Hermitage, Jackson's home near Nashville, Tennessee, and had supported Old Hickory in his battles during the War of 1812. Though Jackson was fifteen years older than Benton, the two men shared the same views about politics, the West and the Union.

Seated before a roaring log fire at Hermitage,

they had long discussions far into the night about John Adams, Thomas Jefferson and John Randolph, friends of both, and about their fears and hopes as England appeared to become more aggressive and threatened to use its sea power against its former colony.

When Jackson's wife, "Aunt Rachel," died, the grieving husband turned to the Bentons for solace. And when he came to Washington as President in 1828, it was only natural that he should open the White House doors to his old friend and his family.

To Jessie, the pipe-smoking, silver-haired man in the White House was affectionate, and an object of admiration. When she and her sisters, playing in a corner of the family sitting room, made too much fuss, Jackson would smile and wave his reed pipe at them in genial admonition.

Jessie felt so at home with the President that she often sauntered away from the circle of ladies and children and went to Jackson, leaning against his knee and delighting in his absent-minded attention. He smoothed her hair with long bony fingers, and when the talks with her father and other men in the group grew animated, the fingers would get tangled in her tresses and pull. But she said noth-

ing, knowing that her father would soon find some gracious reason to free her.

Washington and the big house on Sixteenth Street was a girlhood heaven to the lively Jessie in the 1830's. The house, hidden behind a wall of ivy and scarlet trumpet vine, was built in the best British manner by a Bostonian. It had large rooms with high ceilings, oak floors and wide fireplaces, and was furnished with many choice pieces of mahogany. A garden, playground and coach house were part of the Benton property.

The drawing-room windows looked out in the leafless winters on the Potomac winding toward Alexandria, and she could watch the steamboats and sailboats moving like toys in the distance. On Sixteenth Street the clop-clop of handsome horse carriages intruded on the neighborhood quiet.

Her mother, Elizabeth Benton, a strict Presbyterian, believed in disciplining the children firmly. It was her father, however, who felt that discipline should not be applied to all the children in the same way. He encouraged his wife to adjust it to the temperament of each child, and set the example himself.

Benton treated his children as individuals, with aptitudes and interests that differed. He laid down family rules to promote their physical health, insisting upon plenty of fresh air in the house and daily breathing exercises. The study room and nursery windows were open winter and summer. No matter what the weather, the children enjoyed outdoor play and took walks every day.

They were allowed meat on two days a week only, but otherwise their meals always consisted of milk, fruit and vegetables. "Thus only will you meet life on a calm stomach," Benton would say, disregarding the relatives and friends who thought the Benton table provided a Spartan diet for the children and whose own tables were laden with rich food and drink at every meal.

During dinner the children were allowed to talk of any amusing or agreeable experience they had. If they sulked or pouted, or engaged in unpleasant tales about their companions, they could expect to be punished. Their father didn't believe in sending them from the table "since the unoffending digestion must go on undisturbed." But the offending child would find the next evening that he or she would be eating alone in another room.

It was a tightly knit family circle with a sense of loyalty, beauty and manners that was constantly curried by the considerate parents. After dinner they gathered in the drawing room. Mrs. Benton would work on her needlework by the light of fragrant beeswax and myrtle-berry candles at one side of the blazing fireplace. Benton, on the opposite end, would read under a light he had invented: four spermaceti candles fastened in front of a large sheet of white blotting paper to reflect the light. At a low table close by, the children would work on their exercise books.

Much as she loved the cosmopolitan life of Washington, Jessie was exhilarated each spring by the prospect of visiting the other Benton homes at St. Louis, which her paternal grandmother occupied,

and at Cherry Grove near Lexington, Virginia, the estate of her maternal grandparents, the McDowells.

The trip to St. Louis meant a two weeks' journey by horse-drawn coaches and steamboat. For the overland trip from Washington to Wheeling, West Virginia, where they boarded the boat on the Ohio River, Jessie often was permitted to sit on the box between the driver and her father when Benton decided to take the reins for a time. She would watch with pride as her father skillfully handled the four horses, which were changed at posting stations every ten miles along the route.

Benton told her tales of the Bonny Clabber coun-

try of the Alleghenies, about the busy "Dutch" settlers who built the red and blue Conestoga freight wagons covered with white canvas, which were beginning to move westward beyond the Missouri Territory in a brave quest for new land and new lives. When he saw one of the wagons en route, he would remind her of his own boyhood days in Nashville and the struggle he had taking home goods he had bought for his mother in Louisville in barrels tied three to a horse.

Now, as he urged the horses through the pine forests, across the grass lands and alongside the farms dotted by yellow-green patches of early wheat, he reminisced with old Dan, the driver. Jessie was all ears as she heard her father and Dan exchange stories about snowstorms and robbers, each tale of adventure exciting her imagination and forming memories she would cherish the rest of her long life.

The Bentons would halt at sunset at a wayside tavern. They ate their supper in the noisy crowded dining room. Then the children would be sent upstairs and packed into big feather beds to listen to the click of billiard balls, the scratching of violins as their elders danced a Virginia hoedown, until sleep finally overcame them.

The sun was not yet more than a promising leaden ball in the eastern sky when they arose and breakfasted on ham steak, hominy cakes and milk before resuming their journey toward the Belle Rivière, as they called the Ohio.

St. Louis, on the edge of the frontier, was an enchanting world to Jessie. Her lively eyes swept in the colorful panorama of people in the streets. There were the blanketed Indians; the French army officers in their faded uniforms; priests and nuns; French peasant women wearing white caps, sabots and full red petticoats, with yellow kerchiefs across their white bodices; and adventurers of every description.

In Grandmother Benton's two-story house, surrounded by locust trees with their vanilla-scented blossoms, her father held court. Trappers, hunters, Mexican merchants in gold-trimmed riding breeches and silver spurs, black-robed Belgian businessmen and political allies came and went. Benton was their link to the federal government in Washington. And he was the architect of their dreams of a safe passage to the West with its opportunities for new homesteads and trade.

Benton had an old Army officer teach Jessie Spanish during these Missouri vacations. She already spoke French fluently. When her father would have long talks about the Peninsular Wars, she would be close by. She would help arrange the maps, using beeswax heads for Spanish troops, red wax for the English and black for the French, and listen to the arguments as part of her unique education.

On Saturday she and her sisters had to read their Sunday school lessons, and the next day she would sit beside her father in the family pew at church. When Benton could not be there, she would say, "Alas, my day goes badly."

On other trips to the McDowell estate in Cherry Grove, Virginia, Jessie was delighted to ride in the big coach that was sent to Fredericksburg to meet

the Benton family. It was called "the Pumpkin," and was painted a bright yellow and had many springs. The children loved to ride in it and shouted with joy as they traveled through the Virginia countryside.

The McDowell estate was a park paradise, with its ancient oaks and roadway lined with cherry trees, its maples, sycamores and sea of roses and honey-suckle. Jessie often sneaked away to prowl among the trees and streams, and sometimes she and her sisters sat in the little oak-root house playing a game called "Loves 'n' Hates." Her most frequently mentioned love was "Father" and her pet hate was "saying goodbye to someone you love."

Her father took her quail hunting at Cherry Grove in early autumn days, letting her carry the game bag until it became too heavy. When they paused for rest or lunch, biscuits and apples taken from the deep pockets of his shooting jacket, her father told her stories and read from a small French edition of Homer's *Odyssey*. He would encourage her to translate passages from the book.

The stories he told of Audubon, his artist friend, were best remembered by her. Audubon's courage thrilled her as her father related how he trudged through the canebrakes of Kentucky and climbed tortuous hills to study the eagles, and how he would risk danger in Indian country and suffer from hunger, thirst and insects to watch the birds he sketched.

Grandmother McDowell worried over Benton's concern for Jessie's health and education. The girl spent too much time with her head in books, Mrs. McDowell felt. So she began to show her something of how to manage a household.

Together, they went to the storeroom out beyond the hedges where the day's food supply was selected for the family and servants. They toured the Negro village, a beehive of work in the blacksmith shop, the shoemaker's, the dairy and the weaving cabin where clothes were woven and dyed. Jessie helped gather green walnuts from which brown-green dyes were made, and sumac for red dyes.

Jessie Anne Benton flowered in those summer and autumn days at Cherry Grove. They were part of a childhood that shaped her for the day when she would become detached from her beloved family for the first time.

That day came in 1838, when she was fourteen and the beauty of her face and figure, her intelligence and her gracious manners were already attracting marriage proposals. At a family council the Bentons decided to send her and Eliza to Miss English's fashionable boarding school for girls in Georgetown.

It was a sad blow to Jessie. She pleaded with her father to allow her to continue her studies with him, using every argument and wile available to her. She had read the writings of France's Madame de Staël (who became a famous novelist, political essayist and kingmaker) as a student of her brilliant father. And now she reminded Tom Benton of this.

"I won't need other groups of girls," she implored. "I mean to have no more of society. I only want to study here and be my father's companion as Madame de Staël was hers."

Benton, who felt she needed the company of other young students and the discipline of formal instruction, gently but firmly stood on his decision. Disconsolate, Jessie went off to Miss English's school, to be plunged into a new life and to meet there the man with whom she was to make American history.

2

"Whither Thou Goest . . ."

JESSIE ANNE BENTON'S first encounter with the snobbishness and injustice at school came during the selection of a May Queen. It was her first experience in politics too, and before she was finished she had made a prophet of her mother, who had warned the principal that Jessie was a "Don Quixote" and likely to tilt at windmills in defense of lost causes.

One of her closest friends was Harriet Beall Williams, the daughter of a government clerk, who was an average student and lacked the wealth and social status of those classmates from the homes of senators, Army and Navy officers and propertied gentry. Harriet was tall, graceful, pretty and a talented dancer.

Jessie campaigned for Harriet as May Queen. On election day, Harriet was chosen unanimously by the student body, to the chagrin of the principal and the teachers. Next day, in an arbitrary display that surprised the pupils and angered Jessie, the principal announced that the Queen would be another pupil *she* had selected "more worthy of the honor."

Jessie jumped from her seat. "It's most unjust and unfair," she declared hotly. "The *first* choice was honestly made, and besides the *new* Queen can't even dance."

For her pains, the principal sent Jessie to the infirmary to be treated for "a feverish condition." There, she was given a dose of hot senna tea and kept in solitary confinement for the day.

Jessie was further grieved when Harriet Williams' mother withdrew her from the school. But her despair was short-lived and vindication near at hand. The news came that Harriet was soon to become the bride of Count Alexander de la Bodisco, the Minister from Russia. Harriet a countess! It was a sweet revenge indeed for the May Queen rebuff, and Jessie's triumph became complete when she was chosen the first bridesmaid and stood at the wedding beside Secretary of State James Buchanan and later attended a dinner in the couple's honor given by President Martin Van Buren at the White House.

At the wedding reception Jessie had overheard members of the faculty boasting about the beautiful countess as a much-loved former pupil. Even the headmistress, between sips of punch and nibbles of cake, praised Harriet. All this hypocrisy fortified Jessie for another attempt at persuading her father to let her withdraw from the school.

The conduct of the faculty, she said, caused her a "revulsion of feeling, which makes the thought of going back most unpleasant."

Her father was unconvinced. He maintained that, despite the deplorable attitude of the teachers in their treatment of Harriet Williams, the school provided Jessie with good instruction and much-needed discipline. So again he overruled her. He may have been disturbed but could not have been greatly surprised when later he asked the faculty for a report on Jessie's progress and received the following judgment:

> Miss Jessie, although extremely intelligent, lacks the docility of a model student. Moreover, she has the objectionable manner of

seeming to take our orders and assignments under consideration, to be accepted or disregarded by some standards of her own.

Standards of her own! That was his Jessie all right! Curiously, this school report arrived on the very day that Benton was to meet John Charles Frémont, his future son-in-law.

Frémont's name had been mentioned frequently to Benton by Secretary of War Joel R. Poinsett and by Jean Nicholas Nicollet, the French explorer, both of whom were interested in Western expansion. These two often consulted with Benton, as the one member of Congress wholeheartedly engaged in plans to open the American West.

Poinsett, who had been the American minister to Chile and Mexico, had first met Frémont in Charleston, South Carolina, in the year 1833. Frémont at that time was twenty years old and was teaching mathematics in a private school. The young math teacher was fascinated by Poinsett's own travels in Europe and his life at the court of Czar Alexander of Russia. The two men struck up a warm and immediate friendship.

The Secretary of War discovered that Frémont was well read in the classics, had a good knowledge

of astronomy and was an exceptional student of mathematics. This brilliant young man had a great desire to see the world.

The sloop-of-war *Natchez* under the command of Lieutenant David Farragut was scheduled to sail for South America, and Poinsett obtained for Frémont a post as mathematics instructor to the midshipmen on the cruise. For two years the handsome young Carolinian lived aboard the *Natchez* and absorbed the color and excitement of South American ports. And he became a worshipful friend of the brilliant Farragut.

Back in Charleston once again, Frémont joined the United States Topographical Corps and relished his first taste of the wilderness when he joined a survey party mapping a railroad route between Charleston and Cincinnati.

He did so well on this mission that he was next assigned to a military reconnaissance in the mountainous Cherokee County of Georgia. The mission, in preparation for moving virtually all Indian tribes to new locations west of the Mississippi, was a project of that tough old Indian fighter, Andrew Jackson. Frémont's skill in sketching streams and mountains and other landmarks, his astute reports on the Indians he encountered, his strength and vigor in climbing the steep trails made treacherous by snow and ice, all marked him for the life of a pioneer, explorer, geographer.

Secretary of War Poinsett enabled him to get a commission as second lieutenant in the Topographical Corps, and then ordered him to Washington, where he met the intrepid explorer Nicollet.

Frémont's charm and good looks, plus his intelligence and pleasant manners, made an instant impression on Nicollet, who offered him a chance to join an expedition party headed for the plateau country between the upper Mississippi and the Missouri rivers.

Frémont soon became a protégé of Nicollet. When they returned to Washington to report to War Secretary Poinsett, Lieutenant Frémont was asked to join these men in a call upon President Van Buren.

Nicollet invited Frémont to live with him and with another bachelor, Ferdinand Hassler, superintendent of the coast survey. Hassler had a house on the slope of Capitol Hill, and this became their survey workshop. Nicollet had built an observatory atop the house. Here they studied the stars and drew maps of the region they had explored during their three eventful years beyond the Mississippi.

When Senator Benton called on Poinsett (on the day he had read Jessie's school report) he was already curious concerning the young man so frequently and warmly mentioned by the Secretary of War and the French explorer.

Now in Poinsett's drawing room, Benton and John Charles Frémont met for the first time. Frémont was momentarily awed in the presence of the Senator who held such vast political power. Then he was amazed at Benton's knowledge of the western wilderness — even regions the Senator had never seen.

Benton, in turn, was even more surprised by Frémont. Here was a young man who seemed to share his own dream of the West inhabited by homesteaders; an enthusiastic adventurer who had a solid grasp not only of the many problems involved, but also of the almost limitless opportunities in the challenging West.

They became immediate friends. Benton went to see Frémont's maps at the Hassler House. A few days later, he invited the young man to dinner at the Benton home. There the two younger daughters, Susan and Sarah, were entranced, and twelve-year-old Randolph enraptured, by a guest who had traveled in the land of Indians and buffaloes.

On a second visit to dine with the Benton family, Frémont listened to Susan playing Chopin on the piano and heard Sarah sing English ballads. The next evening he was invited to a concert at the Georgetown school, which the two older Benton girls, Eliza and Jessie, were attending.

While the Bentons and Frémont waited in the visitors' room at the school, Jessie burst in, radiant in a pink candy-striped dress with a rose sash, her warm brown eyes eager to greet her family, and especially her father.

She halted in her rush toward her father as she noticed the handsome young man in uniform stand-

ing nearby. His deep-set blue eyes looked admiringly at her, and his white teeth flashed in a friendly smile. "Lieutenant Frémont," her mother murmured in introducing him. He took her hand, leaned over, and lightly touched it with his lips.

When the more sedate Eliza entered and was introduced, Jessie found herself staring at this socially adept young explorer, already feeling the quick flutter of romance in her heart.

They spoke little as they sat together during the concert. That night, Jessie told Eliza that she thought Lieutenant Frémont was even handsomer than their cousin, Preston Johnson. And she confided that she was glad she wore the pink candy-stripe instead of the dotted muslin with the blue. "It made me look much older," she said.

On that same evening, when Frémont returned to his house, he told Nicollet: "I have fallen in love at first sight. My one thought is how and where I may meet Miss Jessie again."

For a time, Frémont saw her only on occasional weekends when he was invited to the Bentons for dinner. Grandmother McDowell, living with the Bentons during this period, found Frémont a "highly superior young man" and was mainly responsible for the invitations. The family failed to realize how hopelessly in love Frémont had fallen until the inauguration of President William Henry Harrison on March 4, 1841.

At the ceremony, the uniformed Frémont was almost brazen in his unconcealed attention to Jessie. Nicollet was aware of the depth of his friend's emotions, remembering Frémont's own words in describing Jessie after one dinner and an impromptu quadrille he had danced with her in the Benton home: "She has delicacy and winsomeness, alluring gayety with a hint of fire underneath." But Tom Benton and his wife had not been aware of the young man's feelings. Nor did they know that their daughter and Frémont were secretly exchanging love letters.

But now the infatuation was all too clear. When they returned home from the inauguration, the alarmed Bentons called Jessie to the library. In a tone she recognized as grave and final, her father told her that while Lieutenant Frémont was an admirable man, he was also one with "no family, no money and the prospects of slow promotion in the Army. We think him no proper match for you. And besides, you are too young to think of marriage in any case."

Jessie was crestfallen, but her father's tone was

too earnest for her to ignore. Then she heard the bitter verdict: "You are, for a time at least, to see Lieutenant Frémont only on rare occasions. We think it best."

Next day Jessie discovered to her dismay that Frémont also had been informed of the Bentons' distress concerning his attachment to their daughter. He accepted it reluctantly as a hint not to see her for a while.

During the month that followed, both lovers obediently abided by the Bentons' wishes. Then upon President Harrison's death in office, Frémont went to see the Senator to offer the use of the

Hassler house to the Benton family as a site from which to watch the funeral procession. The second-floor workroom, he explained, looked out upon Pennsylvania Avenue and the route of the procession.

Benton considered the offer for a moment. He and Mrs. Benton would be in the actual procession, and Frémont would, he judged, be on duty elsewhere than at home. Jessie and Grandmother McDowell might well be pleased to watch from the Hassler home.

When Jessie and Mrs. McDowell arrived at Hassler's, they found that Frémont had cleared the workroom of its tables, bedecked it with potted azaleas, geraniums and roses, and, on a tea table in front of a blazing log fire, had set out a teapot, cups, French bonbons and cakes.

As Mrs. McDowell looked out upon the raw, cold day, watching the plumed hearse drawn by six white horses move to the somber strains of a funeral march, Jessie and Frémont sat near the fire talking guardedly. Here he proposed to her, and she accepted (but urged that temporarily they keep their betrothal a secret).

Later, the Bentons learned that instead of being on duty, Lieutenant Frémont had been granted sick leave as a result of a slight cold, and that he had played host to Jessie and her grandmother. They now moved with stern determination to prevent the two lovers from any further scheming.

Senator Benton persuaded his good friend, the Secretary of War, to give Frémont an assignment outside Washington. Abruptly, the young lieutenant received orders to proceed at once to the Des Moines River country on a surveying mission.

The lovers were given a half hour together to say farewell. When Benton saw his daughter's forlorn look as Frémont prepared to leave, he partially relented. He told Jessie that if in a year's time she was still in love with Frémont, he would consent to their marriage.

During Frémont's absence, Jessie spent much time at Cherry Grove. Her parents thought she had begun to forget Frémont. "I truly believe our Jessie's childish love affair has quite blown over," Mrs. Benton wrote the Senator.

When Grandmother McDowell died suddenly, Jessie was discovered lying in the garden behind a row of phlox, weeping. Her sister Eliza tried to comfort her by saying their grandmother's death had been an easy one.

"I'm not grieving for Grandmother," Jessie blurted. "*She* was happy. My heart is breaking for *my own* unhappy life."

Jessie struggled to conceal this unhappiness in a series of gay parties. She attended a state dinner at the White House for the Prince de Joinville, son of King Philippe of France, who had, a year previously, brought Napoleon's body back to Paris from St. Helena. Wearing her first Paris ball gown of pale pink muslin trimmed with frills of real Valenciennes, Jessie brushed elbows with President John Tyler and his secretary of state Daniel Webster and the cream of Washington society.

Upon Frémont's return to Washington, the romance sped to a conclusion that startled the Bentons. The lieutenant's successful survey in the Sauk and Fox Indian country won him new respect and dignity.

Watching the two lovers greet each other in the drawing room, the Senator realized that the six months' absence had only strengthened their affections. But he still insisted upon a full year of probation. Frémont and Jessie thereupon decided to elope. On October 19, 1841, Jessie packed a bag for an overnight visit with Mrs. Crittenden, the wife of the Senator from Kentucky, who was conspiring to help the young couple.

She and Frémont were secretly married by a minister who braved the wrath of Senator Benton, but they agreed to wait a while before breaking the news to Jessie's father.

Frémont's mentor Nicollet, lying ill in Baltimore, encouraged his youthful friend to disclose his marriage. But Frémont insisted that "Mrs. Frémont must decide the time."

He broached it to Jessie and suggested, "Let me go to the Senator and explain at once. This is a matter between men."

Jessie had a countersuggestion: "We will explain together."

As they faced Benton in his library, the young man who had risked his life in the midst of prairie fires, Buffalo stampedes and hostile Indians on the prowl was suddenly pale and flustered. He burst out with their secret.

The wrathful Benton exclaimed: "Get out of my house and never cross my door again! Jessie shall stay here!"

He should have known his daughter better than that, for although her love for her father was great, she did not hesitate for one moment. Stepping close to her new husband, and taking him by the arm, she looked squarely at Senator Benton and in calm clarity uttered the pledge of Ruth: "Whither thou goest, I will go; and where thou lodgest, I will lodge: thy people shall be my people, thy God my God."

Benton studied his daughter and saw in her eyes a resolute determination. Then he turned to Frémont in a commanding voice. "Go collect your belongings and return at once to this house." He added that he would prepare Jessie's mother for this startling turn of events.

Not long afterwards, the Senator told a friend: "The thought of my own endless courtship, coupled with the picture of my daughter's felicity, impels me to final approval of this marriage."

Jessie Frémont was seventeen, her husband twenty-eight, and they were a much sought-after couple at the teas, musicales, dinners and balls of social Washington during that winter.

However, the western wilderness beckoned Frémont. The beautiful young bride, brilliant and ambitious for her husband, shared his dreams of opening the trackless way to the Pacific. Her father had made this a national crusade. Now her husband would be the great pathfinder.

Pride and eagerness mingled with sorrow as she braced herself for long separations. Triumphs and heartaches awaited her. As John C. Frémont moved into the era of the Golden West, so in a sense did his young vibrant wife, Jessie Benton Frémont. She was to become his inspiration, working with him during their joyous reunions to record his adventures, then editing every word with her gifts as poet, nature lover and empire builder!

3

Mutiny at Nineteen

ON A GOLDEN spring day in the year 1843, Jessie Frémont walked along the riverbank near her St. Louis home. The green life bursting in the meadows, and the fragrance of jasmine and locust bloom, soothed and lifted her spirits.

Her husband was away on his second expedition into the western wilderness since their marriage. His first foray across the Great Plains and into the Rockies a year before had made him a national hero, acclaimed by the nation's capital and the nation's press for discovering that the plains between the Missouri River and the foothills of the Rockies were not a parched desert, as earlier maps showed them, but a lush prairie, with woodlands and fertile soil — ripe for settlement.

Frémont's study of the face of this wild country, his notes on its flora and fauna, mountains and possible military positions, plus his maps of new routes for emigrants along the Oregon Trail — all these excited Senator Benton and his colleagues in their campaign to expand the country westward.

These ardent expansionists had persuaded Congress to approve a second expedition westward. This one would lengthen the lines of the wagon trails. For Frémont would now cross the big mountains into Oregon country. He also had orders to explore southward, taking a look at California, at this time ruled by Mexico. He would then report on its resources, the attitude of its people, the strength of Mexico's hold on the region, and Britain's influence all along the Pacific coast (for there were many in Washington anxious to extend American power to the Golden Gate).

As Jessie walked along the river, she knew her husband was at Kaw Landing, four hundred miles away, making final preparations for his new venture. The thought of his long absence again saddened her. She turned from the river path and, on a sudden impulse, visited the cathedral. It comforted her.

Starting home, she little dreamed that on this day she would choose to defy the United States government.

On the desk in the drawing room she found a letter postmarked Washington which had arrived by the afternoon boat. Her husband had instructed her to open all mail and to forward to him only the most urgent messages concerning the expedition itself.

The letter was from Colonel John J. Abert, the kindly chief of the Topographical Bureau and Frémont's superior officer. As she read it, she was at first shocked, then indignant. Abert was ordering Frémont to return to Washington at once. He wanted an explanation of why Frémont had obtained a twelve-pound cannon to "defend" a peaceful scientific mission.

To Jessie, Abert's order was not only unfair but mischievous. She detected in it the malice of Abert's scheming son-in-law and his Regular Army cronies who resented Frémont and envied him because of his achievements and fame.

Jessie felt that Abert should have known that the cannon was required for protection against possible trouble with hostile Indians. How could he allow himself to be influenced to the point of believing that the gun was for any form of aggression? The letter trembled in her angry hand. She would not let Frémont's enemies win this spiteful little victory.

She made up her mind quickly. Keeping the contents of the Abert letter a secret, she made contact with a French Canadian who was due to join the Frémont party at Kaw Landing as swiftly as he could cover the distance.

"I have an important message for Lieutenant Frémont," she told him. "How long will you need to get ready?"

The man was moved by her almost distraught condition, by the anxiety and urgency in her voice.

"The time it takes to get my horse," he said. He thought a moment, then added: "But two horses travel better. If I take my brother, he can bring back an answer from the Lieutenant at once."

Agreeing, Jessie wrote out a message to her husband which read simply: "Do not delay another day. But trust and start at once."

Her fear was that Abert might have sent a duplicate letter which would reach Frémont through other channels if he delayed.

In a remarkably short time, the messenger returned from Kaw Landing with this reply from Frémont: "Goodbye. I trust and go."

It was an expression of blind faith in his nineteen-year-old wife's judgment, a token of love and confidence from Frémont. Relieved by the news, Jessie sat down to compose a letter to Colonel Abert, confessing all that she had done.

The strange order was suppressed, she wrote Abert, because he could not have issued it if he had known the facts. If Lieutenant Frémont had received it, good soldier that he was, he would have obeyed it. This would cancel an expedition that had been planned and outfitted at great cost.

Even a minor delay, she continued, would mean that the animals used to transport and feed the men would be deprived of their best season for grazing and would be left underfed for the winter. As for the cannon, she explained that the party needed it in case of attacks from the Sioux, Apache, Blackfoot and other fierce tribes who cared little for scientific expeditions and were only convinced of the need to fight all white men.

She ended the letter with a promise that nobody would know of Abert's order to Frémont except the War Department and herself. It was a bold, impertinent suggestion, and only a woman of great loyalty, love and supreme self-confidence would have dared this kind of defiance.

Not until she had posted her reply to Abert did she begin to realize that her desperate action to save her husband's name and his expedition might be construed as mutiny against government orders. Her father, Senator Benton, was on a political tour, so she had no one in whom she could immediately confide her fears.

During the wakeful nights she spent until her father's return, there flashed through her sensitive and emotional mind the memory of the courage and endurance Frémont had been called upon to display during his exploration of the previous year.

She knew every detail. For while Frémont had been the actual explorer, *she* was responsible for the vivid, highly readable prose that made his adventures come alive to the average American citizen.

In the midst of his own effort to complete his report, Frémont had exclaimed in frustration: "This blasted writing is driving me mad. I can't put one thing on paper the way I want to convey it. If only I could dictate it!"

Instantly, Jessie cried, "Dictate to me. I would love to write it!"

Thus she began a writing career that would flourish in her later years. At nine o'clock each morning, her husband would begin to relate his experiences to his delighted young wife, tumbling out the risks, dangers, triumphs, thrills, setbacks. From this mass of material, Jessie polished into finished form an almost poetic guidebook for pioneers.

As a child she had read the tales of earlier pioneers, Lewis and Clark and Zebulon Pike among them. Her mind was filled with these images as her husband spun his own account. Those who then read the Frémont report could almost see and feel the grassy prairies rolling off to the horizon, the herds of buffaloes grazing the plains, the towering snow-clad mountain peaks and domes of quartz brilliantly touched by the sun. They could follow in their mind's eye Frémont's movements along the silver-crusted sand of the riverbanks, across valleys carpeted with wild flowers (carefully catalogued and pressed into books later to be identified).

Her pen flowed with a smooth rhythm as she wrote about the many other experiences of Frémont's first expedition.

Upon reaching Fort Laramie, he had defied the advice of everybody in his party, including the brave guide and friend Kit Carson who warned him that the Indian tribes were on the warpath and looking for scalps. His courageous determination to push westward despite all dangers soon won Carson and most of the others to a trusting loyalty in his leadership and his cause.

He had risked his life on the icy mountain slopes and experienced hunger for many days. The party's rubber boat had capsized in the boiling rapids of the Platte River and much of their valuable equipment had been lost. They had slept on rocks for want of a softer bed.

On one snowy summit, Frémont had unfurled

a special flag he carried, a flag with thirteen stripes on which the eagle's talons held an Indian peace pipe instead of arrows. This design was ordered by Frémont to show the Indians he might encounter that his intentions were peaceful.

He had, on a crag in the Rockies, watched a bumblebee light on the knee of one of his companions. His imagination was so stirred by it that he called it a pioneer and fancied that it was the first of its species to cross the mountain barrier. He caught the bee and placed it between the leaves of a book in which he had pressed flowers he had discovered for cataloguing in the report he would later make of his journey.

After a winter's work, the report was finished. The Congress was so impressed by it that one thousand public copies were ordered printed. As a result, thousands of new pioneers poured westward along the Oregon Trail.

All of this came back to Jessie in a rush of remembered scenes she had so faithfully recorded. So did one other event of the year before, the birth of their first child.

She had hoped it was going to be a son. She had chosen the name, John Charles Frémont. But the baby was a girl, named Elizabeth after Jessie's mother. She was disconsolate for a time. "This is the first hard blow my pride has ever sustained," she told her husband.

He comforted her with a gift, the faded, wind-tattered flag he had unfurled in the mountains. He laid it across her bed, and said gently: "This flag which I have raised over the highest peak of the Rocky Mountains I have brought to you."

When Senator Benton finally returned to St. Louis, Jessie was prepared for the worst. She told her father about the Abert letter and her defiance of it. Ruefully, she promised that she would accept whatever penalty was in store for her in punishment for her actions.

Her father now surprised her. Instead of condemning her for her act of insubordination against the federal government, he was more outraged against Frémont's superior than she had been. He wrote Abert a bitter letter protesting the attempt to break up the Frémont expedition. He said he would be responsible for his daughter's suppression of the letter ordering Frémont to return to Washington.

In the autumn of that year, Benton went east to Washington, leaving Jessie to supervise the household and to care for her invalid mother. Jessie often read aloud to her mother, whose favorite poem was William Cullen Bryant's *Thanatopsis;* and when the invalid and the baby, now called Lily, were both safely asleep, the young Mrs. Frémont would walk in the streets of St. Louis, in those days teeming with emigrants.

The river city bustled with pioneers of every race and creed. They came on boats that now arrived hourly, and they outfitted themselves for the trek westward at the thriving emporiums of grocers, clothiers, wagon makers and dealers in horses, mules and oxen.

One day Jessie, walking along the river, saw an emigrant wagon in a meadow. She was attracted by the word "Delaware" painted in blue across its canvas top. A young woman of nineteen, Jessie's own age, was seated on an overturned tub nursing her baby. The woman had gay blue eyes beneath her pink sunbonnet and long wavy yellow hair. She and Jessie struck up a conversation, but Jessie did not tell the woman who she was.

"Wouldn't you and your folks like to come along?" the woman asked. "There are three wagons of us. Did you know you can get a whole section of good land to yourselves and save your children from a life of wages?"

Jessie replied, "I can't go because of my sick mother, but how I wish I might." Tears welled up in her eyes, and she walked quickly away.

Relating the incident in a letter to her father, she expressed her longing for her husband in these words: "If it weren't for mother, I would take Lily and go with them. I am strong and not afraid, and waiting grows harder every day."

That winter, Benton had spared his beloved Jessie from a rumor that Frémont had pushed his way into the Sierra range and winter had closed in on him.

The young wife, not hearing from her husband, ıssumed he was on his way back to St. Louis. She

spent her time perfecting her Spanish, sewing clothes for herself and Lily, caring for her mother, entertaining an endless stream of visitors.

When March came, she began setting the table for Frémont's supper and preparing a bed for him each night, expecting him home momentarily. A lamp was left burning in the window. But summer came, and still no word from her husband.

Jessie suffered an alarming loss of weight during this period, but she maintained her cheerful vigil each night. In early August, while she was away one night visiting a sick cousin, Frémont *did* return home.

Though Jessie almost fainted when her husband swept her into his arms, their reunion was a joyous one. Frémont was worried over Jessie's fragile and pale appearance. He knew, however, that when they went to Washington and began to put on paper the account of his latest exploration, she would be restored to full health.

He was right. Back in the capital, Jessie relived with Frémont the hazards and the triumphs of the expedition's struggle across the Rockies, into Oregon and thence southward over the Sierras and down the Sacramento Valley, where a Captain Sutter received the haggard pioneers at his fort. There Frémont learned how weak Mexico's hold on California was, a fact that would shape his career.

The party eventually reached Los Angeles (then a proud adornment of the Mexican empire), after sweeping down the San Joaquin Valley and across the torrid Mojave Desert. Frémont made the return trip across the Great Divide from the great Salt Lake instead of retracing his steps along the Oregon Trail.

Frémont's laurels multiplied. The Senate, which had printed one thousand copies of his first report, now approved the publication of ten thousand copies of the second. General Winfield Scott decorated and promoted him to captain with the words: "Frémont has returned with a name that goes over Europe and America."

In the midst of these honors, Jessie almost forgot her defiance of Colonel Abert's order. But she was reminded of it when the Colonel, still chief of the U.S. Topographical Bureau, invited the Frémonts to dinner. "I go into that house with trepidation," Jessie told her husband. "Perhaps Colonel Abert hasn't buried the hatchet and is waiting to punish me tonight."

Her fears were unfounded. Abert was courtly and gallant and seated Jessie on his right at the table, and never mentioned the incident during the whole evening.

For the next few months Jessie was consumed with the plans of her father and her husband to map new emigration paths to the Pacific. Washington's hopes to acquire the whole Pacific slope were still secret, but growing, and it needed accurate maps and scientific information to replace what Frémont called the "fact and fable map" compiled haphazardly by trappers and travelers.

The day James K. Polk, the Tennessee congressman, was inaugurated as President of the United States, the Frémonts were guests at the White

House. Jessie renewed her friendship with Mrs. Polk, a tall, dignified young beauty who much admired Captain Frémont and his lady. Jessie confided in Mrs. Polk her husband's desire to lay the groundwork for the acquisition of California as American territory.

Jessie turned her energies to this plan. She dined with Daniel Webster and other influential figures in Washington, constantly encouraging the idea that San Francisco and other Pacific ports should be part of the United States. Her knowledge of Spanish led Secretary of State James Buchanan to entrust her with translation of confidential correspondence reaching high officials concerning Mexico's situation in California. Buchanan distrusted a department staff member who usually did the Spanish translations, and he leaned more and more on Jessie.

When Texas accepted American terms of annexation in July, 1845, Jessie's work became crucial. She was busy translating articles from the Mexican press, hostile and incendiary, and watching for those signs which might indicate whether Mexico would invade Texas as a rebellious province or agree to peaceful negotiations.

These were exciting days for Frémont's young wife, but she knew that events were hastening the day when her husband would be off on his third exploration of the West. This time it would be longer than the previous two, lasting nearly two years, and it would lead him into Mexican-held California territory at a time when the United States and Mexico might be at war.

Frémont's new expedition was approved by Congress, and together with Senator Benton and Secretary of Navy George Bancroft, his course was secretly drawn, with President Polk's complete approval.

The evening before Frémont departed, he sat with Jessie as she sewed a waterproof pocket designed

to carry valuable papers. They were in a sentimental mood when he suddenly admitted that he wished she could go along with him to the Pacific. His boyish lament made her laugh through tears she could not restrain.

She wiped a few drops from the new leather pocket, threw her head back and said: "There! That's properly dedicated, and I must be willing to dedicate you to this service which fits you. You leave us to execute plans my father has worked for all his life. You both are a part of me. My work is to let you go cheerfully."

In the months that followed his departure, Jessie took the place of her invalided mother as the hostess at intimate dinners to which the great and near-great were invited. Fur traders and river-traffic managers mingled with foreign diplomats, and the table talk ranged the world. One night after dinner, Jessie remarked upon the fatigue she felt, then said: "No wonder I am tired. We had soup in Washington, the entrée in Mexico and dessert in Belgium."

Among the many guests was Samuel F. B. Morse, inventor of the telegraph, who was grateful for Benton's aid in getting funds voted by Congress for the thirty miles of telegraph line he was building between Washington and Baltimore. General Sam

Houston, newly elected as a senator from the new state of Texas, also came to dine and to recall the days he spent as a corporal under Benton in the war of 1812.

War with Mexico now increased her anxiety over Frémont's safety. In June, 1846, she received letters and messages informing her that he was in Monterey, where the Mexican General Castro's forces were massed in an attempt to drive the Frémont expedition from the country. A Frémont letter to the American consul-general Larkin at Monterey was published, and Jessie read it with apprehension. It said to Larkin:

> From the heights where we are encamped, Gavilan Peak, we can see with the glass, troops mustering at St. Johns. I would write you at length if I did not fear my letter would be intercepted. We have in no wise done wrong to any of the people, and if we are hemmed in and assaulted, we will die every man of us under the flag of his country.

The love of Jessie Frémont for her husband, who had been promoted to lieutenant colonel a short time before, grew with each passing month. Snatches of a long letter she wrote Frémont on June 17, 1846, revealed the bond of mutual affection they had built. She told him of reading about Ponce de León's search for the fountain of youth and then she recalled a letter he had written her soon after their marriage.

> . . . you wrote me: "Fear not for our happiness. If the hope for it is not something wilder than the Spaniard's search for the fountain in Florida, we will find it yet." I remembered it word for word although it was so long since I read it. Dear, dear husband, you know how proud and grateful I am that you love me. We have found the fountain of perpetual youth for love, and I believe there are few others who can say so. I try very hard to be worthy of your love.

Later in the letter, she told him about requests from editors for his biography and likeness, but confessed that she did not know his age.

"How old are you?" she wrote. "You might tell me, now I am a colonel's wife — won't you, old papa? Poor papa, it made tears come to find you had begun to turn gray. You have suffered much and been very anxious, 'but all that must pass.' "

She ended her warm, chatty letter, "I have not had so much pleasure in a very great while as today.

The thought that you may hear from me and know that all is well and that I can tell you again how dearly I love you makes me as happy as I can be while you are away . . .

"Farewell, dear, dear husband. In a few months we shall not know what sorrow means. At least, I humbly hope and pray so." She signed it: "Your own affectionate and devoted wife, Jessie B. Frémont."

She could not then have known that sorrow lurked in the shadows of Frémont's brilliant career. Sinister events were building up in California that would push her husband to the edge of disgrace.

4

"... Seeking the Golden Fleece"

"KIT CARSON to see Miss Jessie."

Jessie laid down her pen and hurried to the drawing room. There, with his friendly blue eyes smiling from under the broad-brimmed felt hat he had forgotten to remove, stood her husband's loyal scout and guide. The rugged frontiersman was dressed not in the clothes of scout and explorer, but in a black broadcloth suit and a clean white shirt.

Jessie kissed him on the cheek, took his hat, seated him in a chair. "Now tell me everything. How is the Colonel?"

In the way of the slow-talking Western man, Kit Carson seemed reticent. Colonel Frémont was well and busy with his duties in Los Angeles, he informed Mrs. Frémont.

Realizing that Kit was not yet ready to tell her the story of her husband's trials in California, Jessie tactfully waited until they had shared dinner.

Then she learned that her forebodings were well founded. The tales she had heard about the Colonel's troubles were all she had imagined.

Puffing on his pipe and sipping a glass of brandy, Kit Carson related the grim account of service intrigue that had caught Frémont. He knew Jessie's pride in her husband was invincible — strong enough so that he did not need to soften his story.

Colonel Frémont, Carson related, had led his bedraggled battalion into Los Angeles in triumph. Through the orders of Secretary of the Navy, George Bancroft, he had been converted from a scientific explorer into an officer in the Regular Army. He had routed the Mexican forces under General Castro in a brief battle and had signed a peace treaty at Cahuenga Rancho before crossing the plain and reaching the Plaza of Los Angeles.

Navy Commodore Stockton, acting under orders received from Washington, dated July 22, 1846, assumed control as commander in chief of all forces in California. He appointed Frémont governor of

the civil administration set up to control the newly acquired territory.

A short time later, General Kearny arrived in Los Angeles, fresh from his narrow victory over the Mexicans at Santa Fe, and attempted to take over the command from Stockton. He demanded that Stockton cease all civil-government operations. Frémont was ordered by Kearny to discontinue the making of appointments without Kearny's approval.

In the face of this dispute between Stockton and Kearny, Frémont chose to honor his relationship with Stockton, who was (as far as Frémont could determine) still the commander in chief. Therefore he flatly refused to obey Kearny's orders.

Californians in the south continued to recognize Frémont as governor while those in the north looked upon Kearny (now established in Monterey, over a hundred miles north of Los Angeles) as *their* governor.

The devoted Carson could not have known the full story of what had happened since he left California bound for Washington. But what he told Jessie was disquieting enough.

"There must be some way to get to the bottom of this," she said. "Your story justifies Colonel Frémont in his position. Would you go with me to call on the President tomorrow?"

Looking at "the plucky and proud" wife of his superior, Carson said he would be honored. Before their afternoon appointment at the White House, a letter arrived from Frémont further explaining his decisive action. Frémont asked that the letter be delivered to President Polk without delay. Reading it, Jessie was fortified for her audience with the President.

Describing the "hostile attitude" between Stockton and Kearny, Frémont had written the President:

The country [California] has been conquered since September last, and General

Kearny had been instructed to "conquer the country." Upon its threshold his command had been nearly cut to pieces and but for the relief of Commodore Stockton would have been destroyed. As to his instructions, how could he organize a government without proceeding to disorganize the present one?

Then in a passage that stirred afresh Jessie's deep respect for the integrity of her husband, Frémont wrote:

You are aware that I had contracted relations with Commodore Stockton, and I thought it neither right nor politically honorable to withdraw my support. No reason of interest shall ever compel me to act toward any man in such a way that I should afterward be ashamed to meet him.

Carson was amazed at the calmness of Mrs. Frémont as they proceeded to the White House. He could not know that she had found new and needed strength for this crisis. She had spent the morning enjoying a leisurely breakfast, chatting pleasantly, without a sign of inner tension. She had been attentive to her ailing mother and patiently listening to her daughter Lily's recitation of her French lesson.

When she emerged from her room, she was dressed in a green cashmere gown, and wore a small green-corded hat atop her brown hair. She turned slowly to get her mother's approval of her ensemble. With a buoyancy that pleased the nervous Carson, who had never previously visited the White House, Jessie flung her cape across her shoulders and announced: "Mr. Carson and Mrs. Frémont will now have a glass of sherry before going into battle."

President Polk received them cordially. But when he had read Frémont's letter and heard Jessie's beseeching question, "Doesn't Colonel Frémont's course seem reasonable in this case?" the Chief Executive hesitated. The sensitive Jessie leaped to the immediate conclusion that the President quite possibly sided with Kearny against her husband.

Polk was evasive, however. "The misunderstandings may by now be settled," he said, "and the recriminations ended."

Her true feelings carefully restrained, Jessie smilingly thanked the President for receiving her and Carson, and departed. As she and the frontier scout walked down the White House steps, she

said: "The President is *always* evasive. Before you leave, we will see him again. If possible, I want Colonel Frémont to have assurances, *not* evasions from us."

After a suspenseful week, Jessie and Carson returned to the White House for a second visit, and this time she sought a straight promise that Colonel Frémont would be kept on duty in California. All Polk would say was that Carson would return with orders to Frémont offering him the choice of remaining on the Pacific coast or rejoining his regiment, the Mounted Rifles, then engaged in the war against Mexico.

Jessie entrusted to Carson a personal letter to her husband. In it she poured out her true and passionate reactions to President Polk's evasions and her great concern regarding Frémont's troubles with Kearny:

> My dear husband: Kit Carson is waiting to take a letter to you. Nothing I can say will express in the littlest degree the love and yearning in my heart — the grief that I cannot be with you. It hurts too much even to write. Besides I would not make you unhappy by my repining. Kit will tell you everything. I am sending you myself — in

miniature. I lay with it over my heart last night. I pray you wear it over yours until *le bon temps viendra.*

Your devoted wife, JESSIE

What Jessie did not know at the time, and did not learn until weeks later when she had returned to St. Louis with her family and Senator Benton, was that General Kearny had tricked Frémont into an act of mutiny and insubordination. For General Kearny had official orders from Washington in his possession which gave him authority to assume the governorship of California. Those orders were dated June, 1846, a full month earlier than the orders on which Commodore Stockton had acted in naming Frémont governor.

But the devious Kearny had withheld from Frémont the fact that he had these official orders until months after his first dispute with the young colonel.

When Kearny finally confronted him with the orders, Frémont offered to resign from the Army. But Kearny, bent on humiliating the young colonel, refused the resignation and ordered Frémont to turn over all his records and prepare to return to Washington. It was not until Frémont reached Fort Leavenworth in the Kansas Territory that he was advised to consider himself under arrest as he continued his journey.

This was the story Senator Benton told his aggrieved daughter as they walked along familiar paths beside the river. Jessie was shocked, but took her emotions in hand to spare her mother and Lily from the whole sordid episode. Senator Benton promised he would go to Washington and demand a court-martial to clear his son-in-law's name.

The night before Benton left, however, Jessie's iron control crumbled. Months of anxiety and fears finally overwhelmed her. She collapsed into a weeping spell that bordered on hysteria. Her father, who had watched her flower into a beautiful and gallant woman with qualities of strength and courage that touched a deep well of pride within him, now tenderly consoled her.

He wrapped her in a warm blanket and brought her a drink he had prepared of milk and brandy. This gradually restored her composure. It was one of the rare times Jessie Benton Frémont would permit herself the luxury of an emotional release from the pressures that had built up inside her.

Jessie, eager and restless for her husband's arrival, took her maid Nancy to the Kansas Landing upstream to await Colonel Frémont. For several days in the August heat, she would stand for hours on the log wharf, waiting with a patience that won her the admiration of the dock hands and roustabouts who knew who she was and called her "the Missy."

Frémont's arrival was greeted by villagers carrying a flag and shouting "Frémont! Frémont!" He could barely push his way through the crowd to greet Jessie, who threw herself into his arms with a cry of joy.

Despite the stories of big trouble that had preceded his journey home, Frémont and his happy wife traveled downstream to St. Louis to sympathetic cheers from every river-town wharf. His entrance into St. Louis was triumphal, and Jessie was almost swept off her feet by the surging crowd at the gangplank. Frémont had to speak a few words of greeting to the throngs before they would allow him to pass.

Upon their return to Washington for the court-martial, Jessie and Frémont managed to steal a few days' vacation. Senator Benton had gone to Norfolk to summon witnesses for the trial. Jessie confided to her sister Eliza: "We are going to mutiny until Father returns to whip us back into line. He doesn't realize that though this trial is important, it isn't everything in life."

The reunion of the two lovers was best told by
Jessie herself in something she wrote much later:

> For a week we lived alone together on a
> happy island surrounded by a sea of troubles.
> We arose late and had breakfast in our room
> before the fire. After the mail came we went
> for a walk or a visit with friends. We even
> drove in the moonlight out to the school in
> Georgetown and looked up at the back win-
> dow where the Colonel's first love letter had
> come up, hidden in a basket of laundry.

Jessie sat through the court-martial in Washington, in those November days in 1847, with stoical

calm. Her hands often trembled with cold and even the heavy gloves she wore could not warm them. Even though her family urged her to stay at home because she was expecting a second child in the coming summer, she insisted on being near her husband during the trial. She attended every session, proud, affectionate, absorbed.

Frémont was found technically guilty on all counts against him, save that of mutiny, by the military court. Senator Benton, Navy Secretary Bancroft and other important figures urged President Polk to set aside the court's verdict. The President chose instead to approve the verdict but to cancel any penalty and to order Frémont back to active duty.

This was unacceptable to the proud young colonel, who felt the verdict was unjust. Now, for the first time, Jessie witnessed a quarrel between her beloved father and her equally beloved husband. Senator Benton urged Frémont to accept the President's order and to work within the service to strike back at his enemies.

Amazed at his father-in-law's attitude, Frémont replied angrily: "I want justice, not official clemency. Would you have me admit the justice of such a verdict?"

Unless completely vindicated, Frémont declared,

he would resign from the service. Jessie struggled with her loyalties. Her father seemed to take for granted that she agreed with him. But then, as later, Jessie chose to stand by the man she loved. When he had thought it over and decided to resign, Jessie defended the decision with a fervor that a doting, understanding father dared not rebuke.

It was March, 1848, and the thirty-five-year-old Frémont and his wife, private citizens again, worked together to finish the report of his last assignment for the Topographical Bureau — his ill-starred venture into California that had brought him further fame and a court-martial.

Jessie was as pleased with this report as with the previous ones, especially with her husband's description of the topography of the San Francisco Bay area. The picturesque opening, through which all ships must enter and leave, he had named the Golden Gate on his maps, a name that would endure. The Senate ordered twenty thousand copies printed of the Oregon and California map.

The year lengthened into a momentous one for the young wife. One day in April her husband rushed into the room, a boyish grin on his face, his eyes alight, the despair of the court-martial erased. He had received a letter from Senator Benton in

St. Louis advising him that a group of influential business men were interested in mapping a south-central railroad route to the West that could be kept open through the winter months. They were anxious to finance Colonel Frémont on an expedition to start in early autumn.

This time Frémont announced to his wife, "There will be no more long separations." After the birth of the baby, she would go to California via the Isthmus of Panama to meet him there. On July 24, 1848, Jessie gave birth to a son. She wanted to name him John Charles after her husband but Frémont insisted upon the name Benton, in honor of the Senator.

As she recovered, Jessie could think of little else besides her impending trip to California. Her dreams of a future beyond the vast mountains were to be realized. She would break with a world of parental love, the civilized and cultured East, the ease and comforts of a life she cherished.

But, to the dauntless Jessie, the world beyond the Rockies was new, challenging the valor and imagination of strong men and women who were unafraid to break with the past. And beside her there would be the man she loved, a man of firm purpose who was always tender to her and who never betrayed her trust in him.

At the moment when her spirits were highest, another cruel stroke was dealt Jessie and her husband. Amid Frémont's preparations for his trek to the West, the nurse rushed to Jessie's door, yelling in alarm, "We can't wake the baby."

In the nursery, the apprehensive mother found Lily in a nightdress, leaning over her brother's crib, trying to warm his cold hands. Jessie took the infant in her arms, wrapped in a blanket, and sat stunned until the doctor arrived. The baby had been dead for several hours of "a defective heart," the doctor said.

Jessie sat silent, uncomprehending. The doctor gently moved to take the baby from her. "The baby is dead, my dear. Let me have him." He bent over to take the child, but Jessie, a soft smile on her face, too grieved for tears, checked him.

"I understand," she assured the doctor, "but I have had him such a little while. Please go away, all of you. We'll wait here together until my husband comes."

A messenger was sent for Frémont, who took the child from his bereaved wife. Only then did she weep, and Frémont did not attempt to comfort her with empty words. His gentle presence and great love for her were enough.

To bridge the chasm of grief, Frémont took Jessie with him to a frontier post on the edge of the trackless prairie. There he completed the details of his new venture while she prepared herself mentally for her own trip via New York and Panama to the paradise she saw ahead in California.

Her father had planned to make the trip with her. But now he was in a state of deep disquiet over the growing slavery question. South Carolina's John C. Calhoun had drawn the South together on the slavery issue, and Benton feared that the Union was being threatened by Calhoun's activity.

Benton informed Jessie of his intention to stay behind. But he had arranged for Richard Taylor Jacob, her sister Sarah's husband, to accompany her. Richard had been in California with Frémont and would — as Benton explained to his disappointed daughter — deliver her safely to her husband.

In New York's Astor House, before her departure, Jessie was confronted with the objections of her favorite cousins, the Prestons of Virginia, who believed the trip was too perilous for her. The California gold rush was in full swing, and fortune hunters clogged New York awaiting transportation on the first available boat.

Benton was indignant concerning the protests from the Prestons. "Who is making war on Jessie Anne?" he demanded as he entered the room unexpectedly. "I won't have her made war upon!"

"But she has never been so far away from home," one of the cousins said.

"There must be a first time in all experience," Benton replied.

"But she doesn't know what lies before her."

"Do any of us here know what the next hour holds?" the Senator argued.

"But Jessie is not strong."

"Not in body, perhaps," Benton said, "but she has the kind of strength that counts in this case — a sturdy spirit. We have already seen it tested."

This argument, Jessie recalled later, made her feel like a nun "carried into the world for the last time before taking the veil: all the pros and cons, old fears renewed, old griefs opened up, the starting made harder than ever."

She also was plagued by another matter. A young Negro who wanted to marry her maid Harriet had reported to an abolitionist group in New York that Mrs. Frémont was about to carry a free citizen out of the country against her will. An irate official of the group met with Jessie while Harriet, in tears, pleaded with her mistress to help her decide her course.

Jessie said that Harriet was free to stay if she wished. And the relieved maid, who had anticipated Mrs. Frémont's decision, immediately produced a happy substitute servant. The incident brought home to Jessie the heightened tensions caused by the slavery dispute.

Aboard the Pacific Mail steamer, Jessie discovered the sea, its solitude, its sense of space and freshness, its power and majesty. They were "healing necessities" to her.

A storm, on the second day out, threatened to founder the boat. However, the weather cleared, and the journey was otherwise uneventful until they reached teeming Chagres Harbor in Panama. There, a ground swell swung the boat about in a wild gyration before it dropped anchor. The captain tried to persuade Jessie to stay aboard and return to New York rather than proceed to shore in the small boats which lacked even gangplanks with which to board them.

He painted a dismal picture of the rancid quarters ashore, the dangers of riding muleback along

treacherous trails, and the great risk of Chagres fever. Jessie was not impressed by the captain's efforts to dissuade her, not even when he confided that he did not wish to be responsible to her father and her husband for "what I feel certain will be your fate if I put you ashore here with your child."

Richard Jacob, seasick as well as homesick, supported the captain. But Jessie simply thanked them for their concern for her safety and Lily's and announced she was determined to go ahead.

The captain resignedly cautioned her: "Don't drink unboiled water. I only hope there's a boat in from Jamaica with sheep, yams, and plantains."

Lily was handed down the ladder to a boatman, and Jessie followed. The small bobbing boat took them to the waterfront, about eight miles away. The stench of stale fish, tar and cinnamon almost overwhelmed Jessie. But her keen sense of adventure delighted in the babel of languages she heard from the passengers — flowing French, soft Spanish and the harder sounds of the Anglo-Saxons. Her eyes feasted on the jungle growth along the water's edge, the green mass interspersed with white and scarlet flowers.

When they reached the shallows, they were loaded into small canoes manned by naked Negroes

and Indians. Now Jessie was almost as frightened
as Lily, who trembled as she clung to her mother's
hand. Fortunately, another captain appeared looking for Jessie. He informed her that she was to go
up the river in a boat owned by the steamship
company. On this slow but sturdy craft she would
be much safer.

For three days, the Jamaican crew poled the boat
against a heavy current. Sometimes they had to
jump out to hack away the jungle growth with long
knives to permit the boat's passage. Their gay
jargon, half song, half speech, as they slashed their
way through the jungle fascinated the well-bred
lady of Washington's salons and made her forget
any discomfort.

Jessie was further buoyed up by the historical
significance of the route she was now taking. "Along
this highway," she wrote, "the buccaneers and revo-
lutionists urged their cayugas, by it the despoilers
of Peru carried their loot to the Atlantic on the way
to Spain." She saw herself now as "among these
other Argonauts upon its waters seeking the Golden
Fleece."

When they arrived at Gorgona, Richard was close
to collapse with a touch of the sun as well as sea-
sickness. A steamship company official ordered him

put in the company's lodging house, to stay there until he could get passage back to New York. He begged Jessie to stay too. But once she learned he would be given good care, she decided to move on. She explained to a fellow passenger: "Poor Richard has been ill from homesickness all along. He has never been a tonic for my courage, and he has now become a pull on my patience."

Before embarking on the mule trail, Jessie had breakfast at the mayor's home, one she would never forget. It consisted of baked ringtail monkey and boiled iguana, a large lizard. It was tasty, she re-

called, "once you forgot the monkey's resemblance to a child burned to death."

The mule train to Panama furnished a series of hair-raising experiences and mishaps. Part of Jessie's baggage was placed on a mule and part on a cow far ahead in the procession. Jessie rode another mule directly behind the one on which Lily was strapped. The trail often narrowed to four feet in width, hanging to the very edge of steep mountain slopes. With no bridges across narrow streams, the mules would put their feet together and jump the water, sometimes depositing the rider in a crashing heap in the stream. At night the travelers slept in Indian huts or tents.

The sunrise gave Jessie one of the few compensations of an otherwise rugged journey. She described it glowingly:

> From the mountain top we looked down upon an undulating sea of unknown blossoms sending clouds of strange perfume into the freshness of the morning. And from the last of the peaks we saw, as Balboa before us had seen, the Pacific at our feet. We felt at home with the Pizarro of Prescott's history — those family readings! — in a time that seemed so far back now, for it lay before this date which would hereafter mark all things.

When they finally reached Panama, she and Lily were carried through water on the backs of Indians. The walled city with its ancient cathedral, its roof and spire inlaid with mother-of-pearl and gleaming in the bright sun, seemed as unreal as a dream. In the square were thousands of gold-rushers heading for California, but just now stranded and bitterly lamenting their luck.

Jessie and Lily found lodgings with a Madame Arce, a smiling, compassionate woman who owned a red-tiled house with a sheltered garden and court.

They had, for the first time in weeks, clean beds, palatable food and a primitive shower bathhouse. In these pleasant quarters they would spend seven weeks before their ship, the *Panama*, could arrive to take them to California.

It was during her stay at Madame Arce's that Jessie received a letter from Frémont, dated January 27, 1849, and sent via Washington from Taos, New Mexico. Frémont was recuperating in the home of Kit Carson from a badly frozen leg, suffered in the Rockies on what turned out to be the worst of his western expeditions. It had been marked by treachery of his white guides and of the Indians, by starvation and by a fierce winter that claimed the lives of ten men. The letter was a shocking recital of the party's hardships, but it ended on a note that heartened Jessie:

> When I think of you all, I feel a warm glow at my heart which renovates like good medicine . . . we shall yet, dearest wife, enjoy quiet and happiness together. I make pictures of the happy home we are to have, and oftenest and among the pleasantest of all I see our library with its bright fire in the rainy, stormy days, and the large windows looking out upon the sea . . .

On June 4, 1849, the *Panama* moved through the Golden Gate after a nightmarish trip during which Jessie had suffered a hemorrhage of the lungs followed by a fever. She and Lily and another woman passenger had shared sleeping quarters on the deck of the steamer (which normally had quarters for only eighty passengers but had left Panama with four hundred). They had made a tent room by draping a large American flag across the spanker boom on the deck, and slept on iron cots with blankets serving as a mattress.

As she looked upon the San Francisco hills rising steeply out of the Bay, Jessie was thrilled by the sight. Tiers of flimsy tents and shacks of canvas and unpainted planks clung to the hills. A cluttered forest of masts moved in the Bay beside her ship, partly obscured by a fog rolling in from the ocean. A dozen small boats nosed their way from the wharf toward their ship. She heard the signal to drop anchor, and she knew that one long voyage had ended and a new life awaited her on the shore.

5

First Lady of the Golden West

JESSIE FRÉMONT was disconsolate as she awaited the reunion with her husband. Her lively vision of the role of a pioneer's wife, sharing his fortune with vigor and cheer, was now clouded by ill health. The fever aboard ship, and a lingering cough, had left her hollow-cheeked and thin to the point of alarm. Wrapped in a heavy blanket in a bleak San Francisco hotel room, she sat watching a smoking fire of brushwood fagots in a darkly apprehensive mood. How disappointed her husband would be!

Frémont had been delayed at Mariposa Ranch, forty thousand acres he owned, nearly a hundred miles inland from the sea. On his last trip to California he had left three thousand dollars with an agent, instructing him to buy a home site with an ocean view near the town of San Jose. But the agent had ignored the instructions and bought Mariposa, mountain land suitable only for grazing, and a target for predatory Indians.

Frémont was angry at first, then realized he had to make the best of it. The discovery of gold at the nearby Sutter's camp led him to believe his own land might yield some of the precious metal. So he had lingered there to hire Mexican workers, on grub-stake terms, to mine the Mariposa tract.

When he finally reached San Francisco and found Jessie in her frail condition, he was fearful. "You have been ill, you are ill now, my darling," he said, as he knelt at the fireside beside her chair.

Lily, restrained at the door by Mrs. Gray (a kindly woman who had nursed Jessie aboard ship and now agreed to stay with her while she recovered), suddenly broke away and rushed to her father. Frémont pulled up a chair and took Lily on his knee. The little girl said: "You didn't come. Mother almost died. A lady downstairs says she will die."

Frémont's face looked stricken, but Jessie sought quickly to comfort him. "In her innocence, she is partly right," she said softly. "Being away from you is a kind of death. Only with you am I fully alive and well."

Despite Jessie's insistence that she was ready to move to Mariposa and take up her new life, Frémont refused. She would have a home in San Francisco, he decided, and immediately rented a sturdy adobe house recently occupied by an American vice-consul.

He had also ordered, as a gift for Jessie, a six-seated carriage, the seats reversible to make a bed. The cushions were upholstered in Spanish leather. In this wondrous vehicle, Jessie was driven to see her new house, which had comfortable furniture and a gay, but neglected little garden. "This is my home!" Jessie exclaimed.

And this she tried to make it, brightening its furnishings with the help of Mrs. Gray, her companion, cook and housekeeper.

The gold rush had transformed San Francisco into one of the busiest and most colorful ports on earth. And Jessie might have gloried in the fabulous life around her. But the chill winds and fog of the Bay area worsened her cough. Home from one of his frequent trips to Mariposa, Frémont was told by Mrs. Gray that his wife could not tolerate the San Francisco winter. She urged him to move Mrs. Frémont down the peninsula, where it was warmer.

Though dejected by Mrs. Gray's suggestion, and the illness it implied, Frémont said he would discuss the matter with his good friend and colleague, Lieutenant Fitzhugh Beale, who had known the Frémonts in Washington and was now stationed on the Coast. With Beale at his side, Frémont reappeared and courteously confronted Jessie, sitting in the garden.

The two young men bowed to her, and Frémont announced in a courtly manner: "Madame, we have come to entreat you to make a long leisurely journey overland in your carriage with Lieutenant Beale and myself as outriders and with a few minions and scullions for making camp. And if they desert us

for the mines, *we* will turn minion and scullion. My friend Beale makes excellent *pot au feu* when it hasn't too much pepper in it, while I can make a bed of your surrey cushions that will tempt you to sweet slumber. What is your pleasure? The carriage awaits without."

Jessie replied with the same mock formality: "Gentlemen, your offer intrigues me. Pray, let us be off at once." She remembered later that she felt "like a fond mother letting herself be deceived by her two boys."

Though she preferred to stay in the now-cheery adobe house because she was weak and travel would be an effort, she realized that the journey Frémont had proposed was "a desperate remedial measure, and I wanted so much to live."

The journey was, in fact, a tonic. The camping party looked more like a gypsy caravan, as it moved along the rough road to San Jose, than it did a mobile sanatorium. Two Indian handymen, Juan and Gregorio, dressed in gay trappings, led the party with two pack mules. One animal was laden with clothing, the other a clanging assortment of kitchen vessels.

Next came the carriage, drawn by two mules. On its red leather cushion seats sat Jessie, pale, dark-eyed, huddled in a blue Army cape. Beside her sat seven-year-old Lily. Alongside the carriage rode Frémont and Lieutenant Beale, both straight in the saddle, bronzed by the sun, ever solicitous of Jessie as the carriage bounced along the road.

It was the spring season, and Jessie welcomed the clear, deep-blue skies and the sight of wild oats on the hillsides and stands of evergreen oaks that reminded her of the apple trees at home. At night she walked about and watched the men make camp. She took special delight in seeing Gregorio, the Indian, concoct a soup, called *quisado*, of Spanish onion, lamb and sweet red peppers in a kettle that swung over a blazing fire on a tripod of stout green branches.

One evening, when she tried to help, Frémont forbade it. "Your work, madame, has to do with the results of ours: to eat with all the appetite you can muster."

Seldom had an invalid on the pioneer routes of the West been so pampered. After supper the party sat around the campfire, Jessie perched on carriage cushions. Her husband and Lieutenant Beale entertained her and Lily with vivid stories of the sea, of Indian encounters and hunting trips.

Talk of politics occasionally enlivened the camp-

fire scene, and Jessie eagerly joined in with quotations from her father's speeches in the Senate urging California's admission to statehood.

She little realized then that the coming political convention at Monterey would open another exciting episode in her life.

At nine o'clock each night, the carriage seats were turned and placed together to make her a bed. The crackling log fire and the soft munching of the animals lulled her to sleep, and she felt a deep sense of protection with Frémont and Beale bedded down on the ground near the carriage.

In the morning a hot cup of tea always awaited

her. Frémont then would lift her down and carry her to a dressing tent made of blankets, where a jug of hot water, a barber's tin basin, a cake of French soap and clean towels enabled her to feel, as she expressed it, far better than the goddess Diana.

Two months of this outdoor life brought new color to Jessie's cheeks and gradually restored her strength. Her amateur doctors, however, decided that she should stay for a short period with a California family in San Jose while Frémont went on to Monterey to arrange permanent lodgings.

She and Lily moved into the house of the Peralta

family, where she spent a happy interlude teaching Lily Spanish (with the Castilian pronunciation), taking part in evening serenades arranged by the cultured Madame Peralta and her three beautiful daughters, and learning the warm and gay customs of the Spaniards of California.

When Frémont came to take her on to Monterey, she left the Peraltas with a heavy heart but with fresh anticipation for a home of her own.

Monterey charmed her, with its pine-covered slopes rising from the rocky inlets and overlooking the silver-crested bay. Frémont had arranged to rent two rooms in the gracious adobe house of a Madame Castro, the wife of the Mexican general he had defeated in the conquest of California. The irony of it touched Jessie. Frémont assured her that Madame Castro "holds no enmity toward me, although her husband is still exiled in Mexico. She lives here with her little daughter Modesta."

Jessie now found herself confronted with the task of making a new home for her family. Once accustomed to every luxury and a household staffed by maids and servants, she now lost no time in learning to be a housewife. She prepared a list of things she needed in San Francisco, and Frémont went off to fetch them.

The gold rush had lured every able-bodied man, leaving behind scarcely anyone to plant gardens or tend the domestic animals. Fowls, eggs, butter, potatoes and other vegetables were scarce. Their meals at first consisted mainly of rice and beans and canned foods. Fortunately, Gregorio the Indian was kept on as a cook, and he managed to find a laundress, an Indian woman, who washed the linen in the time-honored way — soaking it in cold water, pounding it with soap bark on stones, and rough-drying it in the sun.

A fire in a San Francisco warehouse had destroyed all the Frémont clothing. So Jessie had to make a completely new wardrobe for herself and Lily. This was no small task for a young woman whose only previous sewing tasks had been to roll hems for delicate frillings and to embroider flowers in petit point. But she tackled the job with typical zest. She used a set of cambric underclothes as patterns for herself and Lily, and with the materials Frémont had brought back from San Francisco — cotton-backed satins, merinos and thick muslins — she knelt on the floor over the fabrics and patterns, pinning, measuring, scissoring.

Frémont brought also from his shopping tour an odd assortment of merchandise — Chinese matting

for floor carpets, a pair of New England bedsteads, East Indian wicker chairs, colored china, white curtain material, a teakwood table.

Later, when her "home" had become a rendezvous and a hospitable round table for Army officers stationed in the Monterey area and for other guests, some visitors were surprised. They complimented her on achieving comfort "in this queer place."

Proud of what she had accomplished with such primitive materials, she tried to see her living room as her guests saw it. The windows were curtained with Chinese brocade, a color print of St. Francis hung from the whitewashed adobe walls, and resting on top of the inlaid teakwood table were an old copy of the London magazine *Punch*, a bronze Buddha and a Martha Washington sewing basket. On the floor lay a grizzly bearskin, eyes gleaming in the firelight.

To Jessie, this "queer place" was a home that was practically hand-wrought and therefore precious. One evening, she told a gathering: "Ladies and gentlemen, at first glance you might think this room incongruous, but having made a close study of it, I find it true to the period, Pioneer Forty-nine, worthy elements from all over the world, guarded by a California grizzly."

The Frémont home in Monterey, small, cluttered but comfortable, proved as much a magnet to the politicians, military men and intellectuals as had the salons in Washington and St. Louis. They came to discuss and argue, and to listen to Jessie as she regaled them with the situation in Washington as she learned it through long letters from her father.

Among the visitors were a young captain, William Tecumseh Sherman (a frail but fiery officer whose march to the sea and sacking of Atlanta would later become legends of the Civil War), and Samuel H. Willey, a graduate of Dartmouth and a minister, who knew no Spanish and gratefully accepted Jessie's offer to teach him the language so that he could communicate to his non-English-speaking congregation.

In this period, Frémont discovered a rich vein of gold quartz on his Mariposa land, but faced possible trouble over his disputed title to the mineral rights. Jessie was not impressed by this sudden upturn in her husband's fortune. "Gold isn't much as an *end*, is it?" she characteristically confided to a friend. "It can't conjure comforts, nor an ounce of brain rations. I'm simply famishing for the taste of a good book."

Jessie was more concerned with politics than gold.

Her father, Senator Benton, had staked his political career on opposing the growing slave faction in Missouri. He had written to warn her that the "disunionists are trying to dig a slave tunnel through to the coast. Watch out for that."

The words were unnecessary. For Jessie's parlor had become a center for those favoring California's admission to the Union as a free state. And when the statehood convention opened in Monterey on September 3, 1849, Jessie's keen nostrils could literally smell the air of Washington politics as she sat in the hall to watch the hoped-for triumph over the pro-slavery forces.

"Now, if they have someone here who can make the rafters ring," Jessie whispered to a friend, "I shall feel perfectly at home."

The rafters didn't ring, but the delegates fulfilled Jessie Frémont's hopes. They voted for an anti-slavery constitution. And thus was set in motion an election for governor and state officers.

A self-appointed committee came to see Frémont to persuade him to stand as one of California's two United States senators. Jessie fought to restrain her emotions. Here was a chance for vengeance against the injustices heaped upon her husband by General Kearny and the Army. What a sweet vindication it would be for John C. Frémont to sail through the Golden Gate as a senator from the state in which he had suffered the indignity of Kearny's charges a mere two years before!

The committee argued that Frémont was a logical candidate. They spoke of his explorations that made him a popular hero, of the dignity with which he had faced the court-martial, and of his self-won wealth, acquired from the soil of Mariposa.

Frémont knew that political foes would emerge to question his title to the Mariposa lands, to revive the court-martial charges and to question his acts as governor of the California territory under Commodore Stockton.

But Frémont silenced his foes in a letter to a local Democratic leader. He reviewed all his actions in such trenchant and candid words that, of the seven men seeking a senator's seat, he became the most popular.

On a dark December day, lashed by a storm that made the winter of '49 one of the worst in California's memory, Jessie was reading to Lily in front of the fire when the front door burst open. There, drenched to the skin, stood Frémont, almost breathless with excitement. She was momentarily startled because she thought he was at Mariposa.

"I couldn't wait," he explained joyously. "I've ridden from San Jose to be first to greet Jessie Frémont, Senator's lady from the state of California."

Over a supper of cold beef, biscuits and coffee rustled up by the Indian helper Gregorio, Jessie told her husband, "It will be a happy day for me when I see you in Washington."

Frémont replied: "I am unalterably opposed to slavery, but it will be a happy day for me when I see old black Nancy serving you your morning tea in bed."

The swift upturn in their fortunes gave a new meaning to Christmas of 1849, and Jessie made elaborate preparations for it. Gregorio found a shapely little evergreen tree, and the imaginative Mrs. Frémont planned its decorations.

She rolled tinfoil into soft balls, and from empty sardine cans she had Gregorio cut shining disks which were then painted a bright red to be hung on the tree. The tree glistened with warm cheer in the firelight, and Santa Claus appeared in the person of Colonel Frémont just back from a shopping trip to San Francisco.

He had brought a red cashmere shawl for Jessie, a china doll for Lily, and a large package of candy purchased from a street peddler named Winn. Frémont imitated Winn's shrill pitch, to Lily's delight: "Here is your California candy. It came neither round the Horn nor across the Isthmus. None but Winn can make it. Buy it, taste it, try it."

On New Year's night, the Frémonts embarked for Washington, again via Panama. It was a voyage that tested their pioneering spirit. Jessie was again seized with a racking cold. Frémont's leg, injured with frostbite on his last exploration through the mountains, began to cause him great pain.

Both were carried ashore at Panama on stretchers. The generous Madame Arce, who had befriended Jessie before, again offered her hospitality. An intermittent fever kept Jessie in her bed, and one haunted night she dreamed restlessly of a white horse with a vampire bat on his back flapping its wide wings as it sucked the horse's blood.

When Jessie had been nursed back to some semblance of health, Frémont arranged to have her carried across the Isthmus by four men on a palanquin made of a ship's cot swung on two poles. It was covered and had awning curtains to give her privacy and some protection from the insects and the weather. As they departed, Jessie overheard a villager lament in Spanish: "Colonel Frémont will live, but this poor young thing! To die so far from home and country!" But the villager did not reckon with the resolve of Jessie Frémont. She drank huge doses of coffee and quinine, and upon arrival in New York, was on the mend.

The Frémonts were installed in the hotel suite just vacated by the famous Swedish singer, Jenny Lind. Its long French mirror gave Jessie her first glimpse of herself, and what she saw startled and amused her.

The Senator's lady from the Golden West was pale and emaciated. Her clothes hung straight and shapeless to her ankles, her feet were shod in rusty black satin slippers, and the total effect was that of a hapless emigrant. However, two days of rest and the acquisition of a new wardrobe helped Jessie improve almost miraculously. The return to Washington and the reunion with the Bentons were marked with an exultation which Jessie movingly recalled in her later writing:

No person living understands better than I the term "speechless with joy." Father, mother, all the others in the old home greeting us, our old rooms with their heavenly smells of rose geraniums, old friends greeting us! I took sedate little walks down Pennsylvania Avenue and across the Common in the spring twilight, but I wanted to run and shout, to hug the tree trunks, to drop down on the ground and lay my cheek against the new grass, to kiss the crocuses and wild violets, and to float away upon that misty gray-green cloud of young leaves above me.

Frémont and his fellow Senator from California, William Gwin, had to wait weary months for Congress to debate the new state's final admission to the Union. The decision was made on September 9, 1850, when the President signed the bill. Frémont then took his seat among the political giants of the

time — the infirm Henry Clay of Kentucky, the declining Daniel Webster of Massachusetts and the mortally ill John C. Calhoun of South Carolina.

Frémont's term of office lasted only until March 1851, but in that time he introduced bills covering such matters as land titles, custom duties, provision for a state university and an insane asylum, the release of lands in San Francisco for private settlement, an Indian agent bill and a measure that would provide for the opening of a road across the continent, a dream that he and Senator Benton and Jessie had nourished for many years.

His business interests at the Mariposa ranch, as well as political matters, required Frémont to return to California after Congress adjourned. Jessie was expecting a child in April and wanted it to be born in California. Frémont thought the trip too dangerous for his expectant wife, but she insisted.

"I've thought it all out," she announced, "reliable stretcher bearers with a chair instead of a cot for the land trip, proper foods which we take along, tea equipment and plenty of quinine. And awaiting us there will be the faithful Gregorio." Her prophecy was an accurate one, and the trip was made without accident or sickness this time.

wallet a brightly colored folder containing steamer tickets from San Francisco to Chagres and to France. Jessie hardly knew what to say.

Frémont did the talking: "It will be your first vacation and rest — and well earned. The first rest since you spoke those fateful words, 'Whither thou goest, I will go.'"

6

The Presidential Race

LIFE in 1852 was unimaginably slow-paced, by modern standards. But as she toured England and France, Jessie Frémont could feel with good reason that her life was a roller coaster that touched the stars one moment and descended into a dark tunnel the next.

Just three years before, this twenty-eight-year-old girl had bathed from a barber's basin in a dressing tent made of blankets in the western wilderness of the United States. Now she gloried in a marble tub, watching her bath water flow from the beaks of gilded swans, and dried herself with satin-damask towels in a dressing room lined with mirrors in a romantic house on Paris's famous Champs Elysées.

What a far cry was this from her adobe quarters in Monterey!

She had come to France after a fabulous stay in England. There she had been presented to the Queen at the Court of St. James's. Kitty Lawrence (the daughter of the United States Minister to Great Britain and a friend of Jessie's from their early Washington days) had helped her to learn how to curtsy and had advised her on the gown she needed for the occasion.

The gown was a pale pink moire (over a deep-pink satin petticoat) with a long train, and embellished with a corsage of roses. When the costume arrived at the Frémont suite in London, Lily was allowed to open the box. When she saw the shimmering folds of satin, Jessie's daughter sighed, remarking, "We'll have to send it back. We've got the Queen's dress by mistake."

Her father laid his hand on her shoulder. "We have the Queen's dress, my dear, but there's been no mistake."

As Jessie, her wealth of red-brown hair puffed and curled, her brown eyes aglow, her cheeks radiant, showed off her gown to Kitty Lawrence and Kitty's mother, Mrs. Lawrence turned to Frémont and asked: "Colonel Frémont, did you ever see your wife as beautiful as now?"

Bowing low, Frémont replied: "Yes, madame, the first time I ever saw her."

"But you can't possibly recall what she wore then!" exclaimed Mrs. Lawrence.

"Yes, I can," said Frémont. "She called it a pink candy-stripe. In this gown she reminds me very much of herself at that time."

The enraptured Jessie extended her gloved hand to her husband. "For that, monsieur," she said, "you may kiss your lady's hand and pray she doesn't fall fainting among the folds of her train when she curtsies to the Queen."

Of that moment when Queen Victoria and her Prince Consort, Albert Edward, received this ebullient girl from America, Jessie recalled: "I felt myself not a Democrat bowing the knee to royalty but an American paying homage to a figure of womanly goodness and power."

Standing with the red velvet and gold hangings of the throne for a background, the Queen impressed Jessie as a "beautiful picture." The young American girl looked on as the other women glided toward the Queen, curtsied, and backed off. She

felt as though she were caught in some festive
dream.

> Her gown of white satin and lace [Jessie
> later wrote of the Queen] made her appear
> taller, while the very long red-velvet train,
> disposed in folds to the step below, added to
> her air of majesty. The broad blue ribbon
> of the Garter crossed her breast. Diamonds
> flashed from neck and arms, and gave out
> their light from the crown upon her small
> and graceful head. Prince Albert in a white
> and gold uniform completed this truly royal
> picture.

Among the great figures of English society she
met, the one who thrilled her most was the Duke
of Wellington, now a stooped old man but still en-
veloped in the glory he had won on the battlefield
against Napoleon Bonaparte.

Her meeting with the Duke inspired a rapturous
letter to her father, in which she wrote in part:

> You have often smiled over my "What
> more can I ask of life?" But you will not
> smile when I say it now! I have told you how
> we dine and breakfast and drive in the park
> with personages it is a delight as well as an
> honor to know. I have told you how Colonel

Frémont's reputation makes all our introductions personal and kindly; how Kitty has got me all into gay-colored gowns, saying I must keep away from my favorite violet and gray, for I am too fragile (you know I am not). But I have not told you that your little daughter's eager but undistinguished hand has lain in that of the Duke of Wellington. What more *can* I ask of life?

The niece of the Duke, a Lady Bulwer, had introduced Jessie to the distinguished old warrior. As Jessie related it, they were at a party when Lady Bulwer said to her, "There is my uncle. He is eighty-four and very feeble. Come, I'll present you."

When Lady Bulwer spoke Jessie's name, the Duke of Wellington peered at her for a moment, bowed, and said slowly: "I know that name, a distinguished name." He then took Jessie's hand and pressed it and smiled. "It is well that only a smile was demanded of me!" Jessie wrote her father.

Before leaving for Paris, Jessie was shaken by word from her home that her brother Randolph had died of a malarial infection. Her husband consoled her through a period of deeply felt loss. He implored her not to wear "that grief-reminder, black," and soon had her mind engaged in preparations for the trip to Paris.

If London had put her in touch with her English ancestry, Jessie felt that in Paris her heart was even more at home with the spirits of the Frémont ancestors. "French history, literature, and language," she recounted later, "seem somehow my own. At dinners, the playful teasing banter, the epigrammatic wit are a happy challenge, while the Englishman's pronouncements are more often a thrust."

Her capacity for inspiring quick friendships brought into the Frémont circle the Comte de la Garde, a member of the Bonaparte family and a leader of the French inner circle. When the Frémonts first met the seventy-year-old Comte at a ball, he declared at once that he admired and respected Colonel Frémont for his explorations, but that only his rheumatic knees prevented him from kneeling in passionate adoration of Mrs. Frémont. Thereafter, she became *ma petite* to the Comte, who led Jessie and Colonel Frémont on a breathless round of gay parties.

She drank in the enchanting vistas of Paris from a terrace in St.-Cloud, watching the Seine flowing far below the steep hill and looking out upon the

wooded Bois that was like a glowing flower in the lapel of the city. She watched Napoleon III enter Paris and ride with princely courage through the streets, threatened by demonstrators who were cowed by the Emperor's royal bearing and fearlessness.

And her personal charm and the quiet dignity of her husband once again turned the Frémont drawing room into a salon for newly won friends. They captivated the French, except on one occasion when Jessie was giving a small party to celebrate her husband's fortieth birthday. Her dinner guests entered the drawing room which had been gaily decorated

with Colonel Frémont's favorite flowers, heliotrope and white roses. But just before dinner was served, Jessie was advised that the servants below stairs were packing to leave at once.

It turned out that Frémont's birthday was on the same anniversary as the death of King Louis XVI, and the servants were legitimists who would not stay in the same house that was "celebrating" the death of their revered monarch. Jessie rushed to explain that she was celebrating, not the King's death but her husband's birthday. The servants were finally placated and consented to stay.

In February, 1853, Jessie gave birth to another child, a dainty girl who was named Anne Beverly after Frémont's mother. The Comte de la Garde called her *petite Parisienne*. Shortly after the mother had recovered from her confinement, Frémont received news from Washington that persuaded him to return as soon as possible.

Frémont's claim to the mineral rights at the Mariposa Ranch was still unsettled. Debts incurred while he was governor of California remained unpaid by the government, despite promises in Washington to clear them up. But more important, perhaps, was the content of a letter from his father-in-law, the redoubtable Thomas Benton. In it Benton said that Secretary of War Jefferson Davis was planning to appoint some West Point officers, with no experience, to head up a government survey to report on the best railroad route to the Pacific.

This was a natural task for Frémont, Benton wrote. Since the government was determined to disregard him, Frémont must organize an independent survey equipped and led by himself.

Back in Washington (with French maids who refused to leave the Frémonts' employ, so attached had they become to the American family), Jessie settled down for another long separation from Colonel Frémont. The nation's capital was boiling with ferment over the slavery issue. Benton's refusal to compromise on the issue had eventually lost him his Senate seat, and now he had time to lecture and begin to write — with the aid of his talented daughter — his memoirs entitled *Thirty Years' View*.

While Frémont completed preparations for his latest western expedition, tragedy again stalked Jessie. Her baby Anne died of a digestive ailment. When her father commented on Jessie's calmness through the ordeal of death and burial, Frémont was moved to remark: "It was she who remained dry-eyed to comfort me, for I was unmanned over the cruelty of this bereavement. Her calm stoicism, so superior to mere resignation, soon shamed me into control."

Frémont's new expedition was no less arduous than earlier ones. At one point during his absence, Jessie underwent an odd psychic revelation. She had been brooding through long wakeful nights, and her health was again being sapped. A young cousin, Susie, came to visit her and to spend the night. When Jessie went to an adjoining room to get firewood, she felt a light touch on her shoulder and strangely heard Frémont in the room, laughing as he whispered, "Jessie . . . Susie." Hurrying to

the other room, Jessie found Susie in a half-fainting condition. The incident was both alarming and uplifting, for now she knew that her husband, with whom she was so closely attuned, was somehow safe from immediate danger. Later, upon his return, Frémont checked his notebooks and calculated that at the moment Jessie felt his "presence," he was arriving in a Mormon village after leading his party over hazardous slopes and defiles. A slight mistake in direction and the party would have missed the village and starved in the winter snows of the mountain passes.

Discussing the uncanny nature of the phenomenon with Benton, Frémont said: "It doesn't seem strange to me. With each so much a part of the other's thoughts and feelings at all times, a crisis with either might cause these thoughts to materialize into a sense of actual physical presence."

In May 1854, Jessie was compensated somewhat for the loss of the baby Anne by the birth of a son, whom they named Frank Preston after a favorite cousin. Not long afterwards, the shadow of death again darkened her life. Her mother, long a patient and beloved invalid, finally fell into a deep sleep from which she did not awake.

Thomas Benton's unselfish devotion to his invalided wife had become a cherished tradition in the politics-hardened world of Washington. Never a complaint issued from his lips during her long illness. Her loss left him broken and bereft of a love that sustained him in his bitter political battles with those who talked secession and threatened a breakup of the Union he had fought to preserve.

When the Benton home caught fire and burned to the ground a few months later, the old man was prepared to forsake Washington, now a seedbed of dissension. Jessie readily agreed, for she had long wanted to live in New York. By the spring of 1855, she was receiving letters from her Southern cousins, bitter, accusing notes: "Are you and Colonel Frémont with us, or are you following your father's views, so *strange* for a Southerner?"

That summer, with Frémont back in California to deal with squatter trouble at his mine, Jessie took the children with her to Nantucket, where she abandoned her cares and joined the children and their playmates to make small boats, build castles in the sand, and to tell stories of the sea and adventures shared with her husband.

One day during this interlude, she displayed her talent as a child psychologist. Lily came running to her to announce that "Charley said two 'damns' when the castle tower fell. Young Sears taught him. Shall I send him home?"

"No, bring them both here," said Jessie. With the penitent little boys in her presence, Jessie said to Johnny Sears, a neighbor's child: "If you like to swear, Johnny, why don't you swear as the Quakers do? Come, I'll teach you and Charley."

She brandished a finger at young Sears and said in mock anger: "Thee's a little *thee!* Thou!" The small boys were delighted with these queer-sounding "oaths" and practiced them with manly diligence. Lily, however, wanted to know from her mother "what about those 'damns'?" Jessie whispered to her daughter, "Let's forget them."

To Nantucket that summer came S. N. Carvalho, the famous artist and daguerreotypist who had accompanied Frémont on his last expedition and who had become the first photographer of western exploration. Carvalho planned to write and illustrate a book of his own about the Frémont expedition. The artist caused Jessie to swell with pride as he described Frémont. Reading from a rough manuscript, Carvalho said of her husband that

> . . . in that long gamut of hardship and suffering his heroic quality sang above the minor

jangle of despair . . . Personal courage and
skill he showed at all times, and his high
qualities of fairness to subordinates. Through
every vicissitude his self-control, his endurance of spirit against obstacles won from us
a kind of worshipful loyalty. The Colonel's
worst enemies grant him personal courage.
We can prove all our claims from actual suf-
fering with him.

Those qualities of mind and heart attributed to
Frémont were to propel Jessie into the 1856 campaign for the Presidency of the United States. Frémont had already been sounded out by influential
Democrats when he arrived at Nantucket to rejoin
his family.

On the terrace of the seaside cottage, Jessie was
serving the children at a tea table, and Frémont
stopped unobserved to watch them. His wife was
garbed in a light blue gown with a ribbon around
her head. On Lily's lap sat chubby, pink-cheeked
Frank while Charley stood against his mother's knee.

"As I watched that family picture," Frémont recalled later, "I longed for the power to make it the
symbol of my Jessie's future, but already I had come
to impart disturbing knowledge."

What Frémont had to tell Jessie was that the

Democrats wanted him to run for the Presidency but that he would have to endorse the fugitive-slave law. For a free-soil Democrat to accept this would forever brand him a traitor to principle and life-long belief.

To return to Washington as the mistress of the White House! The prospect quickened Jessie's breath. Scenes of her childhood raced through her mind — a six-year-old clinging to her father's hand as they strolled through the great rooms of the Executive Mansion, looking in the state dining room with its tables laden with pastries and giant salmon embedded in a sea of meat jelly, leaning against Andrew Jackson's knee in the White House sitting room on a sunny day as his gnarled fingers ran fondly through her hair.

But only for a moment did these memories tempt her. Compromise her husband's dedication to his great conviction — a nation free of slavery? Never! They had discussed the matter on a long evening's walk to Lighthouse Hill in Nantucket. "With clasped hands," Jessie remembered, "we made our decision and turned homeward with the kindly beacon at our back."

Frémont was destined to be a presidential candidate anyhow. For the Republican Party had been formed by free-soil advocates and had blossomed into a potentially powerful group, with the support of New York's William H. Seward and his Whig followers. These Republicans turned to Frémont as a candidate in 1856. Once again he and Jessie had to decide. This time it was not so simple.

Her seventy-four-year-old father, a lifelong Democrat, opposed Frémont's acceptance of the honor. He was sure the Republicans were hoping to gain Benton's endorsement of a ticket headed by Frémont. But Benton, true to his own beliefs, refused and advised Frémont that he would publicly oppose his son-in-law if he ran for the Presidency.

Jessie's abiding love for her father caused her to hesitate. But Frémont won the day when he told her, "Your father will be compelled to respect the honesty of our decision, though he will never agree to the wisdom of it."

So it was. Frémont was nominated at the convention in Philadelphia in June. And the Frémont house at 56 Ninth Street in New York became a campaign branch office, mail station, press clipping bureau and buffet lunch room, open eighteen hours a day. Jessie Frémont presided over it tirelessly, with tact, patience and grace.

She was besieged by those who demanded inter-

views, favors, advice. To her library came Henry
Ward Beecher, a Protestant clergyman famous for
his dramatic sermons, to outline a series of speeches
he would make in Frémont's behalf. Other distinguished citizens also came to offer their help. One
visitor, however, did not come to enlist in the Frémont cause but to ask harsh and impertinent questions about the Frémonts.

She was a militant newspaperwoman who opened
her interview by rudely announcing: "You're not as
sensible looking as the cartoons make you out. Are
you prepared to speak truthfully about the slaves
you had in Washington as body servants and about
the girl you tried to entice to California?"

Jessie contained her surprise at such impertinence,
and calmly explained that the freed slaves had
stayed on voluntarily and happily with her family.
They were pensioned off when they grew too old to
work. She told of the maid who was left behind in
New York to marry her sweetheart, and of the new
red silk dress she had given the girl for the bridal
ceremony.

The questions came thick and fast — did she read
profane literature on Sunday, were her children
obedient, how many had died and of what? When
Jessie ordered tea served, the newspaperwoman

proved relentless: "I see you ape the English by serving tea and cake between meals."

Jessie was unabashed. "I *am* English in the tea-hour tradition," she said. "I find it a comforting break in my full and often wearying day."

"But you have it served by a French maid," the reporter scornfully persisted, looking at the girl who had refused to leave the Frémonts in Paris.

Lowering her voice in a confidential manner, Jessie said, "Yes, but between us, I think I make a better tea myself. I had no maid in Monterey. I heated the water in a long-handled iron saucepan over a smoky fire. Instead of cakes, I lifted a sardine from a crowded can and gave him a decent burial between two soda crackers."

The remark brought laughter from her tormentor, who finished her tea and departed amicably. When Frémont heard of the interview, he was indignant and asked why Jessie "didn't show her out?"

"Ah, my dear," his wife replied, "you didn't *see* her. I would as soon think of snubbing Napoleon's aide." Jessie's patience and forbearance were rewarded, for the woman wrote a friendly article praising the Republican candidate's wife as a fine woman and housekeeper who could cook over a campfire.

The campaign was a bitter one, filled with acrimony and innuendoes about Frémont's religion, hinting at questionable parentage, dredging up old controversies. It fell to Jessie to make written answers to these charges, and she wrote them with courage and skill and taste. For she knew no other way.

Henry Ward Beecher reported to Jessie that half the women in his congregation were copying her hair, dress, her manner of speech, her walk. Jessie found, wherever she went, that young women were gowned in her own favorite violet and white muslins, with her favorite flower at their belts. Letters came to her revealing that infants throughout the nation were being named Jessie Anne.

There was great heartbreak too in the heated campaign. Her father was declaring the Republican Party a menace to the Union, a sectional movement that stirred sectional hostility. "Do the people believe the South will submit to such a President as Frémont?" Benton was saying on the platform. "We are treading on a volcano that is liable at any moment to break forth and overthrow the nation."

Her love for her father, however, was too strong and too understanding to be diminished by these words, which caused her great anguish but which did not prevent her from writing to him about his grandchildren and inquiring about his health.

Frémont had his champions: Wendell Phillips, the Boston orator, reformer and abolition leader; Carl Schurz, the German-born editor active in the anti-slavery movement; Schuyler Colfax, prominent member of Congress later to become Speaker of the House and a Vice-president of the United States under Grant, and a little-known Illinois lawyer named Abraham Lincoln. Frémont also had won the loyalties of such famous literary figures as essayist Ralph Waldo Emerson, novelist Washington Irving and the poet John Greenleaf Whittier. But his cause was foredoomed. The fears of the slaveholders and the ambitions of the secessionists were too great. The Democratic candidate, James Buchanan, who walked the path of compromise and strove not to alienate any faction, was elected.

Though disappointed for her husband, and deeply discouraged by the "trial of mud" through which he had to campaign, Jessie took defeat with characteristic fortitude. She had been greatly touched by the homage the people had paid to her, by the flattery of their imitations and their warm toasts to "our Jessie."

To a friend who had come to console her, she had

replied, with a gallant laugh: "I'm very glad that all my little Jessie Annes are too young to weep over the discovery that they are *not* the namesakes of a President's wife."

The following spring, when Frémont was called again to California to take care of his Mariposa Ranch interests, Jessie packed the children and sailed for another visit to France. They lived an idyllic life in St.-Germain-en-Laye for several months, returning to find Thomas Benton a virtual ghost of his former self.

Benton's devotion and tenderness to his children was heroically demonstrated in this period. He knew he had cancer, but he had sworn his doctors to secrecy. "My daughters are young mothers," the old man had said, "they shall not be subjected to the prolonged anxiety and grief over my illness."

Jessie's thirty-three years had been crowded beyond belief with excitement, heartache, triumphs and disasters, good fortune and bad. But bright and glowing like an inextinguishable lamp was the love between her and her father, matched only by the mutual bond that existed between her and her husband — a bond on which she would solely rely through new griefs and joys that lay ahead.

7

"From the Ashes of His Campfire, Cities Have Sprung"

THE VILLAGE of Bear Valley, in Mariposa County, was a daguerreotype of the Wild West come to life. Its single street was lined with a double row of saloons, its single hotel had bedrooms partitioned by sheets of tin. A meal of corned beef and flapjacks was an elegant repast. And its people were hard-hewn miners and Indians and Mexicans and ugly-tempered squatters.

On a hill above town, Jessie had converted a squalid adobe shack into what she called the "White House," with canvas walls separating the bedrooms, covered with rose-trellised wallpaper, a fireplace built in the dining room and a lean-to she had constructed with the help of Biddle Boggs, a lanky

Pennsylvanian who served her as a handyman and watchman.

Here she was called upon again to display a pioneer fortitude and adjusted herself quickly to many minor hardships, including the lack of fresh meat and vegetables and the absence of many of the comforts of living in the East. And here it was that she learned in the most casual manner of her father's death. Frémont's lawyer and his wife had come to her cottage on horseback one day, and the woman, while still astride her horse, remarked upon how gay and cheerful Jessie seemed.

"Why not?" Jessie asked. "I am very well now."

"Oh, so soon after your father's death — "

Hearing this, Frémont moved quickly to his wife's side. "Is my father dead?" she asked. His answer was a wordless one. He gathered her in his arms, tears in his eyes. He had learned this disturbing truth from a letter received a few days previously but had wanted to shield Jessie as long as possible. Now he reproached himself for not telling her sooner, for Jessie was taking the blow with great courage.

Later she said of her father, "His memory is for me to worship, not to weep over."

It was here in the West that Jessie learned first-hand something of the heavy burdens her husband carried in his long struggle to protect his rights to the Mariposa mines.

The squatters were fighting, intermittently, to seize possession of the Black Drift, one of the richest veins on the Frémont property, and the nights were often shattered with the sound of exploding bombs made of tin cans filled with gunpowder. One day while Frémont was away Jessie received an eviction order signed "Dinis O'Brient, President," ordering her out of their house within twenty-four hours.

This kindled the Irish in her. Leaving Boggs to guard the premises, she and Lily drove to the Bear Valley inn. She showed the eviction notice to the landlord and asked him to deliver a message to "O'Brient." She would stay on her property, come what may, and if her house was burned down, she would camp on the grounds and dare anybody to move her.

Impressed by her courage, the innkeeper poured two glasses of wine and insisted that "Tom Benton's daughter" join him in a drink. That night Jessie slept in the cottage while Boggs kept watchful guard against possible intruders. After a few days, the trouble subsided and a committee of valley women rode out to the "White House" to thank the Colonel's wife for standing her ground.

"If you had been driven out, our hills would have run blood," they told her.

It was early in 1859 that the "White House" was visited by a distinguished guest, Horace Greeley, the famous New York editor. With only three days in which to prepare, Jessie decided to tailor a "new" wardrobe. She took two frayed cashmere dresses, several worn underskirts and a linen dress shirt of Frémont's, and with flying needles managed to make attractive garments for herself, Lily and Charley.

As they sat before the fire on his first night as a guest, Greeley said to Frémont: "I was prepared for your enormous development here and seeing you in good health from successful work, but I expected to see Jessie Anne a worn, if not a resigned little recluse, living on bacon and greens. What I see is French frills and blue sash ribbons, and what I eat is good rolls and French-made dishes."

The Bostonian Richard H. Dana, who had achieved fame with his book *Two Years Before the Mast,* also came to the little house above Bear Valley, to lighten Jessie's heart with such remarks as, "This country is full of colonels, but when people speak of THE colonel, they mean Frémont."

Isolated as she was, Jessie began to grow pallid and restless and to gaze abstractedly as though dreaming of a more civilized life — all of which she vainly hoped to hide from her husband. But Frémont was too sensitive to every mood and manner of his beloved wife not to detect this inner longing she so deeply felt.

He asked Jessie to go to San Francisco with him, and there on a hundred-foot bluff called Black Point, looking out through a dense growth of mountain laurel toward Alcatraz Island in the bay, he showed her the house he planned to buy as a permanent home. "Here are the three things we have always held as requirements for a home: the sound of the sea, a view, and a gentle climate," he said.

Black Point became a happy haven to Jessie, a sea home she loved so much "that I had joy even in the tolling of the fogbell." And it became, as always, a mecca for old friends and new ones, a salon for lively talk, gay parties and distinguished visitors.

At Black Point she met Nellie Haskell, the ten-year-old daughter of neighbors, a shy, sensitive child with a love for music — a girl who would through-out the rest of Jessie Benton's life be a source of comfort and happiness. Nellie had those qualities that her own daughter Lily lacked, a creative imagination and zest for life, an interest in the arts and a great hunger for knowledge. One night, when Lily declined to go to the opera with her mother and the Haskells, Jessie invited Nellie. She drank in the music with an eagerness that pleased Jessie. When Nellie said goodnight, she whispered, "Will Miss Lily care if I love you as much as I like?" Jessie reassured her that Lily wouldn't mind.

Another lifelong attachment was made at Black Point — to the new Unitarian Minister Thomas

Starr King who had come to the Coast from Boston. He was little more than a thin beardless youth, and quite unimpressive to Jessie until she heard his deep rich voice from the pulpit pleading for a liberal Christianity. She also discovered a sharp humor in this frail young man. "Before our friendship progresses farther," he said to her one day, "let me ask: do you think it sacrilegious for a man constitutionally hilarious to become a minister?" When he returned from a lecture tour of nearby mining camps, he said: "I never knew the exhilaration of public speaking until I faced a front row of revolvers and bowie knives."

Starr King would come to the Frémonts, and in a corner of their vast grounds, work on his lectures, and then at tea, try them out on Jessie. She was thrilled by their eloquent appeals to preserve the Union and to abolish slavery. The minister brought another young man to see Jessie, a struggling writer who was discouraged and needed a good listener and friendly critic. It was Bret Harte, a tall, handsome figure who soon became another fast friend of the Frémonts.

Jessie listened to Harte's stories and poems, counseled and encouraged him. "Sometimes her comments cut like a lash," Harte told Starr King, "but her praise is sincere and freely given. To know her is a liberal education." Jessie helped Harte obtain a job in the Federal Surveyor's office so that he might have some security while writing. From that time on, he always called her his "fairy godmother."

It was the autumn of 1860 that the siren call of Washington was again heard by the Frémonts. The Colonel was informed that President-elect Abraham Lincoln was considering him as a possible Secretary of War or as Minister to France. Frémont was not greatly interested in either post, but he asked Jessie's wish in the matter. "Above all, to stay here where I have taken root along with my rosebushes," she said, "otherwise, to do what you think best."

Frémont thought it best to offer his services to President-elect Lincoln in some capacity in case of war. He sent this word back to Washington. Meanwhile, he moved to sell half his Mariposa property to obtain funds to develop the other half, a transaction that required an immediate trip east. Jessie insisted upon staying behind, dimly aware that gathering storms of war would soon envelop the nation.

After a meeting with Lincoln in New York's Astor House late in February, 1861, Frémont wrote to his wife, adding in a postscript, "With the inflammatory

press and inflammatory conversation on every hand, I am convinced that actual war is not far off." Barely a month after Lincoln was inaugurated, the storm broke. Fort Sumter in Charleston harbor was bombarded, the opening salvo of the Civil War.

Through the insistence of Postmaster General Montgomery Blair, who stressed Frémont's Southern birth and Western popularity, President Lincoln appointed Frémont a major general and assigned him to command the Western Division with headquarters in St. Louis. And Jessie rented the Black Point house and hastened to join her husband.

The Reverend Starr King saw her off on the boat.

He left with her a bouquet of English violets plucked from his own garden, and a copy of Emerson's Essays, and this gay farewell: "Smell, read, and rest."

Later, Jessie discovered that Starr King had written a friend of his, "Have you met Mrs. Frémont? I hope so. Her husband I am very little acquainted with, but she is sublime, and carries guns enough to be formidable to a whole Cabinet; a she-Merrimac, thoroughly sheathed and carrying fire in the genuine Benton furnaces."

She needed all the steam her fiery spirit could muster as Frémont took the family to St. Louis, where his command awaited him. The Missouri city, which she had loved as a frontier threshold, now sent a panicky chill through her. Confederate flags were everywhere, the streets were deserted and steamboats lay idly at their wharves. It was a hostile city now, and old friends were openly secessionist.

Jessie volunteered her services to scrounge supplies for the woefully neglected hospital at Jefferson Barracks. To St. Louis came Miss Dorothy Dix, a spinster nearing sixty who had been appointed Superintendent of Women Nurses. Under Miss Dix's supervision, Jessie fought the battle of shortages, especially of nurses. And she had to fight Miss Dix as well, for the prudish superintendent decreed that only "settled and moral" women would be accepted as volunteer nurses. This order shut the door to many willing young women, and Jessie protested: "Since our need is so great, why do you refuse these young women?"

"Would you have no moral standards, Mrs. Frémont?" Miss Dix snapped.

"Standards, yes," replied Jessie with spirit, "but surely in this crisis strong hands and a desire to serve make up for a lack of experience. And as to morals, you and I have both observed that the hand of female virtue often has chilly fingertips."

Miss Dix yielded with a "Perhaps you are right," and the barrier to young volunteer nurses was noticeably lifted.

Meanwhile, General Frémont's command was afflicted by shortages of men and supplies and plagued by guerrillas. Although Missouri had voted in state convention to remain in the Union, half or more of its 160,000 people appeared to sympathize with the South and secession sentiment was a constant torment to Frémont. He had managed to muster only about ten thousand men while at least forty thousand rebels darted about the countryside, capturing horses, food and clothing from Union citizens, burning bridges and wrecking trains, forcing loyal families to flee without their belongings into Illinois and Iowa.

Frémont had been given a free hand in Missouri by President Lincoln. Now he chose to exercise it by issuing a proclamation: All Missouri to be under martial law, all arms and property of those aiding the enemy to be confiscated, and all their slaves to be freed. President Lincoln still hoped to keep some wavering border states within the Union, and Frémont's order came as a shock to Washington. Abruptly to free all slaves at this moment well might drive the hesitant into the rebel camp.

Lincoln sent his secretary John Hay to see Frémont, with a kind letter asking him to modify the proclamation dealing with freed slaves. "This letter is written in a spirit of caution, not censure," the President wrote.

It was not in Frémont's character to back down once he had taken his stand. His act brought some stability to Missouri. But faced with charges of bad judgment, Frémont sent Jessie to Washington with a letter to the President, explaining his actions. Jessie's interview with Lincoln was disheartening. She found him in a hard, disagreeable mood, his

mind set against Frémont for raising the slavery issue so bluntly.

Frémont was eventually removed from his command, but not before he had appointed an unknown brigadier general to command the troops of southeastern Illinois and Missouri. This act also was seized upon by his critics as ill-advised. The brigadier general was Ulysses S. Grant, later to lead the Union forces to total victory and to become President of the United States.

Jessie's life now ebbed and flowed with the fortunes of the war, while her husband was moved to other commands. Eventually he resigned his commission to return to private life when the Army of Virginia was placed under General John Pope (whom Frémont had considered disloyal and insubordinate during the Missouri days).

Her mood in this period was expressed in a letter to her sister Eliza written just after Lincoln had signed the Emancipation Proclamation on January 1, 1863. Her attitude toward the harassed Lincoln had been softened by this act, which she considered a vindication of Frémont's earlier proclamation in Missouri and a refutation of the schemers in his entourage who wanted to protect slavery.

"War-politics — hyphenated heartache," she

wrote Eliza. "My one hope is to see the end of both in our lives. At fifty the General is gray, worn and in poor health. At thirty-nine my heart, played upon by joy and bereavement, pride and humiliation, longs only for the privacy of a real home again . . ."

Among her treasures of these years was a manuscript poem sent to her by the New England Quaker poet John Greenleaf Whittier, written to acclaim Frémont's policy on abolishing slavery in Missouri:

> Thy error, Frémont, simply was to act
> A brave man's part, without the statesman's tact,
> And, taking counsel but of common sense,
> To strike at cause as well as consequence.
> Oh, never yet since Roland wound his horn
> At Roncesvalles, has a blast been blown
> Far-heard, wide-echoed, startling as thine own,
> Heard from the van of freedom's hope forlorn!

One of the most heroic episodes of the war, to Jessie, was the valor of the Zagonyi Guards, a battalion led by a former Hungarian Cavalry officer, Major Charles Zagonyi, under Frémont's command in the fighting at Springfield, Missouri. Survivors of the fallen Zagonyi Guards were destitute, and Jessie felt upon her return to St. Louis that their story should be made public. She secured a commission from the Boston publishing firm of Ticknor and Fields to write a book about them. In the incredibly brief interval of twelve days, she completed the manuscript that launched her upon a writing career that would dominate her middle years. *The Story of the Guard* was the first of the Civil War stories of heroism in action, and it was an immediate success.

As the 1864 elections approached, Frémont came under pressure from influential friends to run again for the Presidency on a third-party ticket that would be composed of radical Republicans, the "war" Democrats and the Unionist Germans. Jessie was apprehensive and indecisive. She had had her difficulties with Lincoln, but now she sensed that the group supporting Frémont were acting selfishly, using him as a tool to undermine Lincoln's candidacy for a second term.

The Frémonts were staying at a seashore cottage at Nahant, Massachusetts, when the troubled Jessie wrote to John Greenleaf Whittier, asking him to visit her. Whittier came as an overnight guest, and frankly gave Frémont his advice. He said he had supported every move of the General until now, but that he felt that Frémont would best serve his country by withdrawing in Lincoln's favor.

"There is a time to do and a time to stand aside," the gentle poet said, and those words ultimately carried the day. Frémont withdrew.

When the war ended, Frémont found an estate in Sleepy Hollow near the Hudson River in New York, where Jessie might draw solace for the longing she felt for San Francisco's Black Point and the home she had cherished most. They called the estate by the Indian name "Pocaho," and it was as ever a magnet for many friends. Here she wrote, rested and discovered a peace she had not known for years. Her three children were the delight of her life.

Lily, now in her twenties, was as her mother described her, "a frank endearing good-nature that is a staff to my tired mind." Charley was a slender, dark-eyed, restless youth who longed for a life at sea, and Frank was studious, a gifted child pianist with dreams of his own. And there was Nellie Haskell, now nineteen, who came to stay at "Pocaho" for long periods. She gave to Mrs. Frémont a sense of companionship and understanding and affection she did not always feel with her own daughter.

Jessie could have happily lived out her years at "Pocaho." Here it was that she saw those she loved grow and prosper. Nellie Haskell was married to the son of a fine old Salem family, Charley graduated as an ensign from the naval academy, and Frank entered West Point. Serene in her own world, she was wholly unaware of Frémont's disastrous business complications. He had kept from her the fact that his ventures were almost hopelessly entangled in railroad bonds of dubious value and that he was caught in a series of lawsuits brought on by tricky associates who had betrayed his trust in them. Now the dark and turbulent fate that seemed to hover in the background of her bright and calm years overtook her at "Pocaho," as it had many times in the past in a seemingly relentless cycle.

Their descent from wealth to near poverty was swift and dizzying. The estate had to be sold, and they were forced to move into a musty house in town. Jessie's countless friends loaned her carriages and horses, a box at the opera, gave her gifts of gloves and books. She accepted them without any loss of pride or feeling of martyrdom. The schoolgirl who had struggled against discrimination of other classmates because they lacked wealth or position had grown into a woman who expected her friends would not turn away from her because of a mere loss of wealth. Money may have been the means to surround herself with comforts, but its loss did not dismay her. Her inner resources had a value far exceeding all the money in the world. "I am like a deeply built ship; I drive best under a strong wind," she said as she prepared to consult with New York editors and publishers to sustain the family income with her writings.

In the years after "Pocaho," she wrote for publication a series of articles for newspapers and magazines, sketches of California and Panama and her journeys to Europe, whimsical stories for children, all of them a prelude to the *Souvenirs of My Time,* a book of her girlhood and foreign travel.

She had another experience with life in the

primitive West in 1878 when Frémont was appointed territorial governor of Arizona by President Rutherford B. Hayes. She was now an old hand at turning adverse conditions into a gay adventure, and she had the added incentive of being able to write of her experiences for publishers eager for every word from the pen of Jessie Benton Frémont. The governor's salary at Prescott, Arizona, was two thousand dollars a year, and Jessie was aghast at how much things cost to live there — ninety dollars for house rent, forty dollars for cook's wages, prohibitive prices for canned goods. There was no fresh fruit at all.

"Though we are beautifully located," she wrote of this experience, "we are four hundred miles from a lemon, and if I were offered the choice of one of my beloved La Marque roses and a fat ripe tomato just off the vine, I should take the tomato."

While the Arizona climate was good for her lungs, the high altitude caused her frequent attacks of vertigo and extreme lassitude. Frémont again determined to see that she was in healthier surroundings. He resigned in 1883 and returned to New York and a home he had acquired for Jessie on Staten Island.

A journalist of the time, William Croffut, visited the Frémonts on Staten Island and wrote that they "were prolonging the romance of half a century before." Of Jessie at this time, the journalist wrote:

> Mrs. Frémont's hair was white as snow, but she showed few other indications of aging, and talked as brilliantly as ever. She greatly resembled her father, even in gestures and manner when animated by conversation, and with lineaments somewhat softened, inherited his studious and logical mind and his commanding spirit. Her sons were both tall, black-haired and bearded like a pard. And both, like their sister, showed strains of Gallic blood, the influence of their grandfather, the poor scholarly French gentleman who came to Virginia at the beginning of the century and found their grandmother in her teens.

During this Staten Island period, Frémont fell ill of a severe case of bronchitis, and the doctors warned that the seventy-five-year-old patient had to go to a warm climate at once. Jessie arranged with an old friend of their wealthier days, Collis P. Huntington, to use his private railroad car to take the General to California. Frémont objected. He appreciated his friend's generous offer, but he simply would not accept it.

Here we were, lovers for forty-seven years, having our first lovers' quarrel! [Jessie wrote later]. The General, thin and pale, sat frowning, staring out the window, answering my questions and protests with the exaggerated politeness I had often seen him use so effectively when angry with the boys. I prepared his favorite chicken broth; he barely touched it. The papers came; he didn't feel like listening to the news. I was perfectly miserable, but whenever I looked at his sunken cheeks, I was determined to see this thing through unless the General refused to stir, and I thought this quite likely as I waited for Mr. Huntington to come.

See it through, Jessie did, with Huntington's assistance. During the trip to California in 1886, Jessie was haunted by a thousand memories. At Manassas Junction, "the years rolled back," she wrote, "to that ordeal of the nation, the time of partings, of unreturning feet, of great aims and great deeds, and in its mighty shadow, personal pain felt rebuked."

But the memories faded into a great moment of current joy when, early in the journey, General Frémont, who had sat unsmiling for a long time,

beckoned Jessie across to his section of the railroad car and took her hand in his. "You were right to come. I feel better already," he said.

With her gift for adjusting to new surroundings, her sense of charity and her love for people, Jessie was soon immersed in the community life of Los Angeles. Her mood was movingly communicated in a letter she wrote in 1889 to John Greenleaf Whittier, recalling the Quaker poet's advice to her husband that night at Nahant, Massachusetts, when Frémont agonized over whether to contest Abraham Lincoln in the 1864 presidential campaign.

"There is a time to do and a time to stand aside," she remembered Whittier saying. "It was a deciding word, coming from you," she wrote.

And how we have outlived all of that time! Here on this far shore where the serene climate gentles even hard memories, I seem to look back into another life, its strifes ended, only its results in good cherished. I have my daughter with me. My other children and the dear young grandchildren I have not seen for two years. It is much that they are well and write me fully and often, but your Angel of Patience is more than ever a part of my life . . .

I am writing by an open window, a La
Marque rose wreathing all the gallery in deep
green foliage and white roses kept well
trimmed back to pillars, and balustrade to let
in the sweet sweet sunshine . . . We are
established here . . . We have many pleasant
friends and take our part in some of the good
works of the town, for there are many up-
rooted families here . . . And I write, hoping
often that I too may find a place in some tired
heart and lead to new courage.

It was not long after this letter was written that
Jessie and John Frémont separated again. The California climate had restored his health and revived
his interest in business opportunities available to
him. And the United States Congress at long last
recognized his services to his country, voting to
restore his rank as major general and grant him a
pension. His presence in Washington was needed
to complete the formalities. He said goodbye to his
wife and struck out for the East — first Washington,
then New York.

He never returned. For after a brief seizure in
New York, he died of peritonitis. His son Charley
was at his side. The news shocked Jessie into a

virtual state of paralysis. Her indomitable will to carry on and to tidy up her life as a distinguished, revered widow sustained her through this emotional crisis.

When she became fully aware of this final separation from her beloved husband, she was obsessed with the thought that some symbolic link between them must accompany him to his grave. She wired Charley asking him to place in her husband's hand before his burial the miniature picture of herself that he had always carried with him since the day in 1845 she had sent it to him by Kit Carson.

"Herself in miniature" would be forever with him and betoken in a small way her abiding love for the man with whom she had shared so much in the history of a nation.

Jessie eased her grief, in a fury of work, by answering letters of condolence from all parts of the globe, by completing unfinished manuscripts left by Frémont, and by continuing her own writing projects. She was determined that history would have an accurate version of those phases of his career that had been distorted by his enemies. She recalled to a San Francisco reporter who had come to see her the words of Greeley that "Fame is a vapor; popularity an accident. Character is the only thing that endures." Time, she said, would vindicate General Frémont.

"I may not live to see his enemies sitting in homage at the unveiling of his statue," she said, "but John C. Frémont's name can never be erased from the most colorful chapters of American history.

"From the ashes of his campfires, cities have sprung."

In her Los Angeles cottage, at the corner of Hoover and Twenty-eighth Streets, Jessie Frémont lived out the rest of her years. She kept apace with the times, and to her door came many distinguished visitors to pay their respects. Among these were President William McKinley and Secretary of State John Hay who had been Abraham Lincoln's youthful secretary. "My goodness, John, how you have grown!" she said to the delighted Hay.

On the morning of December 27, 1902, Jessie Benton Frémont died in a peaceful sleep, at the age of seventy-eight. Her body was cremated, and the urn was taken for burial at Piermont-on-the-Hudson, beside her husband where she would have wanted to be, in death as in life.

Some other books about the FRÉMONTS

William Brandon,
> THE MEN AND THE MOUNTAIN: FRÉMONT'S FOURTH EXPEDITION. *New York, 1955.*

Allan Nevins,
> FRÉMONT: THE WEST'S GREATEST ADVENTURER. *New York, 1928, 1961.*

Irving Stone,
> IMMORTAL WIFE. *New York, 1948. A novel based on the life of Jessie Benton Frémont.*

INDEX

CPSIA information can be obtained
at www.ICGtesting.com
Printed in the USA
BVHW032138240422
635221BV00001B/19